Thanks
for Putting
my thoughts
in order!

Mucho amor
Culer !

Tractatus Logico-Philosophicus

(Logical-Philosophical Treatise)

By
LUDWIG WITTGENSTEIN

With an Introduction by
BERTRAND RUSSELL, F.R.S.

First published London, 1922

This publication: Really Simple Media,
London, 2011

Publisher's note:

This edition of Tractatus Logico-Philosophicus is abridged from the original 1922 edition only in that the duplicate German text has been deleted.

Please advise any non-trivial errors or omissions to:

Really Simple Media
483 Green Lanes
London
N13 4BS

INTRODUCTION

By BERTRAND RUSSELL

MR WITTGENSTEIN'S *Tractatus Logico-Philosophicus*, whether or not it prove to give the ultimate truth on the matters with which it deals, certainly deserves, by its breadth and scope and profundity, to be considered an important event in the philosophical world. Starting from the principles of Symbolism and the relations which are necessary between words and things in any language, it applies the result of this inquiry to various departments of traditional philosophy, showing in each case how traditional philosophy and traditional solutions arise out of ignorance of the principles of Symbolism and out of misuse of language.

The logical structure of propositions and the nature of logical inference are first dealt with. Thence we pass successively to Theory of Knowledge, Principles of Physics, Ethics, and finally the Mystical (*das Mystische*).

In order to understand Mr Wittgenstein's book, it is necessary to realize what is the problem with which he is concerned. In the part of his theory which deals with Symbolism he is concerned with the conditions which would have to be fulfilled by a logically perfect language. There are various problems as regards language. First, there is the problem what actually occurs in our minds when we use language with the intention of meaning something by it; this problem belongs to psychology. Secondly, there is the problem as to what is the relation subsisting between thoughts, words, or sentences, and that which they refer to or mean; this problem belongs to epistemology. Thirdly, there is the problem of using sentences so as to convey truth rather than falsehood; this belongs to the special sciences dealing with the subject-matter of the sentences in question. Fourthly, there is the question: what relation must one fact (such as a sentence) have to another in order to be *capable* of being a symbol for that other? This last is a logical question, and is the one with which Mr Wittgenstein is concerned. He is concerned with the conditions for *accurate* Symbolism, *i.e.* for Symbolism in which a sentence "means" something quite definite. In practice, language is always more or less vague, so that what we assert is never quite precise. Thus, logic has two problems to deal with in regard to Symbolism: (1) the conditions for sense rather than nonsense in combinations of symbols; (2) the conditions for uniqueness of meaning or reference in symbols or combinations of symbols. A logically perfect language has rules of syntax which prevent nonsense, and has single symbols which always have a definite and unique meaning. Mr Wittgenstein is concerned with the conditions for a logically perfect language—not that any language is logically perfect, or that we believe ourselves capable, here and now, of constructing a logically perfect language, but that the whole function of language is to have meaning, and it only fulfils this function in proportion as it approaches to the ideal language which we postulate.

The essential business of language is to assert or deny facts. Given the syntax of a language, the meaning of a sentence is determinate as soon as the meaning of the component words is known. In order that a certain sentence should assert a certain fact there must, however the language may be constructed, be something in common between the structure of the sentence and the structure of the fact. This is perhaps the most fundamental thesis of Mr Wittgenstein's theory. That which has to be in common between the sentence and the fact cannot, so he contends, be itself in turn *said* in language. It can, in his phraseology, only be *shown*, not said, for whatever we may say will still need to have the same structure.

The first requisite of an ideal language would be that there should be one name for every simple, and never the same name for two different simples. A name is a simple symbol in the sense that it has no parts which are themselves symbols. In a logically perfect language nothing that is not simple will have a simple symbol. The symbol for the whole will be a "complex," containing the symbols for the parts. In speaking of a "complex" we are, as will appear later, sinning against the rules of philosophical grammar, but this is unavoidable at the outset. "Most propositions and questions that have been written about philosophical matters are not false but senseless. We cannot, therefore, answer questions of this kind at all, but only state their senselessness. Most questions and propositions of the philosophers result from the fact that we do not understand the logic of our language. They are of the same kind as the question whether the Good is more or less identical than the Beautiful" (4.003). What is complex in the world is a fact. Facts which are not compounded of other facts are what Mr Wittgenstein calls *Sachverhalte*, whereas a fact which may consist of two or more facts is called a *Tatsache*: thus, for example, "Socrates is wise" is a *Sachverhalt*, as well as a *Tatsache*, whereas "Socrates is wise and Plato is his pupil" is a *Tatsache* but not a *Sachverhalt*.

He compares linguistic expression to projection in geometry. A geometrical figure may be projected in many ways: each of these ways corresponds to a different language, but the projective properties of the original figure remain unchanged whichever of these ways may be adopted. These projective properties correspond to that which in his theory the proposition and the fact must have in common, if the proposition is to assert the fact.

In certain elementary ways this is, of course, obvious. It is impossible, for example, to make a statement about two men (assuming for the moment that the men may be treated as simples), without employing two names, and if you are going to assert a relation between the two men it will be necessary that the sentence in which you make the assertion shall establish a relation between the two names. If we say "Plato loves Socrates," the word "loves" which occurs between the word "Plato" and the word "Socrates" establishes a certain relation between these two words, and it is owing to this fact that our sentence is able to assert a relation between the person's name by the words "Plato" and "Socrates." "We must not say, the complex sign 'aRb' says 'a stands in a certain relation R to b'; but we must say, that 'a' stands in a certain relation to 'b' says that aRb" (3.1432).

Mr Wittgenstein begins his theory of Symbolism with the statement (2.1): "We make to ourselves pictures of facts." A picture, he says, is a model of the reality, and to the objects in the reality correspond the elements of the picture: the picture itself is a fact. The fact that things have a certain relation to each other is represented by the fact that in the picture its elements have a certain relation to one another. "In the picture and the pictured there must be something identical in order that the one can be a picture of the other at all. What the picture must have in common with reality in order to be able to represent it after its manner—rightly or falsely—is its form of representation" (2.161, 2.17).

We speak of a logical picture of a reality when we wish to imply only so much resemblance as is essential to its being a picture in any sense, that is to say, when we wish to imply no more than identity of logical form. The logical picture of a fact, he says, is a *Gedanke*. A picture can correspond or not correspond with the fact and be accordingly true or false, but in both cases it shares the logical form with the fact. The sense in which he speaks of pictures is illustrated by his statement: "The gramophone record, the musical thought, the score, the waves of sound, all stand to one another in that pictorial internal relation which holds between language and the world. To all of them the logical structure is common. (Like the two youths, their two horses and their lilies in the story. They are all in a certain sense one)" (4.014). The possibility of a proposition representing a fact rests upon the fact that in it objects are represented by signs. The so-called logical "constants" are not represented by signs, but are themselves present in the proposition as in the fact. The proposition and the fact must exhibit the same logical "manifold," and this cannot be itself represented since it has to be in common between the fact and the picture. Mr Wittgenstein maintains that everything properly philosophical belongs to what can only be shown, to what is in common between a fact and its logical picture. It results from this view that nothing correct can be said in philosophy. Every philosophical proposition is bad grammar, and the best that we can hope to achieve by philosophical discussion is to lead people to see that philosophical discussion is a mistake. "Philosophy is not one of the natural sciences. (The word 'philosophy' must mean something which stands above or below, but not beside the natural sciences.) The object of philosophy is the logical clarification of thoughts. Philosophy is not a theory but an activity. A philosophical work consists essentially of elucidations. The result of philosophy is not a number of 'philosophical propositions,' but to make propositions clear. Philosophy should make clear and delimit sharply the thoughts which otherwise are, as it were, opaque and blurred" (4.111 and 4.112). In accordance with this principle the things that have to be said in leading the reader to understand Mr Wittgenstein's theory are all of them things which that theory itself condemns as meaningless. With this proviso we will endeavour to convey the picture of the world which seems to underlie his system.

The world consists of facts: facts cannot strictly speaking be defined, but we can explain what we mean by saying that facts are what make propositions true, or false. Facts may contain parts which are facts or may contain no such parts; for example: "Socrates was a wise Athenian," consists of the two facts, "Socrates was wise," and "Socrates was an Athenian." A fact which has no parts that are facts is called by Mr Wittgenstein a *Sachverhalt*. This is the same thing that he calls an atomic fact. An atomic fact, although it contains no parts that are facts, nevertheless does contain parts. If we may regard "Socrates is wise" as an atomic fact we perceive that it contains the constituents "Socrates" and "wise." If an atomic fact is analysed as fully as possible (theoretical, not practical possibility is meant) the constituents finally reached may be called "simples" or "objects." It is not contended by Wittgenstein that we can actually isolate the simple or have empirical knowledge of it. It is a logical necessity demanded by theory, like an electron. His ground for maintaining that there must be simples is that every complex presupposes a fact. It is not necessarily assumed that the complexity of facts is finite; even if every fact consisted of an infinite number of atomic facts and if every atomic fact consisted of an infinite number of objects there would still be objects and atomic facts (4.2211). The assertion that there is a certain complex reduces to the assertion that its constituents are related in a certain way, which is the assertion of a *fact*: thus if we give a name to the complex the name only has meaning in virtue of the truth of a certain proposition, namely the proposition asserting the relatedness of the constituents of the complex. Thus the naming of complexes presupposes propositions, while propositions presupposes the naming of simples. In this way the naming of simples is shown to be what is logically first in logic.

The world is fully described if all atomic facts are known, together with the fact that these are all of them. The world is not described by merely naming all the objects in it; it is necessary also to know the atomic facts of which these objects are constituents. Given this total of atomic facts, every true proposition, however complex, can theoretically be inferred. A proposition (true or false) asserting an atomic fact is called an atomic proposition. All atomic propositions are logically independent of each other. No atomic proposition implies any other or is inconsistent with any other. Thus the whole business of logical inference is concerned with propositions which are not atomic. Such propositions may be called molecular.

Wittgenstein's theory of molecular propositions turns upon his theory of the construction of truth-functions.

A truth-function of a proposition p is a proposition containing p and such that its truth or falsehood depends only upon the truth or falsehood of p, and similarly a truth-function of several propositions p, q, r...is one containing p, q, r...and such that its truth or falsehood depends only upon the truth or falsehood of p, q, r... It might seem at first sight as though there were other functions of propositions besides truth-functions; such, for example, would be "A believes p," for in general A will believe some true propositions and some false ones: unless he is an exceptionally gifted individual, we cannot infer that p is true from the fact that he believes it or that p is false from the fact that he does not believe

11

INTRODUCTION

it. Other apparent exceptions would be such as "p is a very complex proposition" or "p is a proposition about Socrates." Mr Wittgenstein maintains, however, for reasons which will appear presently, that such exceptions are only apparent, and that every function of a proposition is really a truth-function. It follows that if we can define truth-functions generally, we can obtain a general definition of all propositions in terms of the original set of atomic propositions. This Wittgenstein proceeds to do.

It has been shown by Dr Sheffer (*Trans. Am. Math. Soc.*, Vol. XIV. pp. 481–488) that all truth-functions of a given set of propositions can be constructed out of either of the two functions "not-p or not-q" or "not-p and not-q." Wittgenstein makes use of the latter, assuming a knowledge of Dr Sheffer's work. The manner in which other truth-functions are constructed out of "not-p and not-q" is easy to see. "Not-p and not-p" is equivalent to "not-p," hence we obtain a definition of negation in terms of our primitive function: hence we can define "p or q," since this is the negation of "not-p and not-q," *i.e.* of our primitive function. The development of other truth-functions out of "not-p" and "p or q" is given in detail at the beginning of *Principia Mathematica*. This gives all that is wanted when the propositions which are arguments to our truth-function are given by enumeration. Wittgenstein, however, by a very interesting analysis succeeds in extending the process to general propositions, *i.e.* to cases where the propositions which are arguments to our truth-function are not given by enumeration but are given as all those satisfying some condition. For example, let fx be a propositional function (*i.e.* a function whose values are propositions), such as "x is human"—then the various values of fx form a set of propositions. We may extend the idea "not-p and not-q" so as to apply to simultaneous denial of all the propositions which are values of fx. In this way we arrive at the proposition which is ordinarily represented in mathematical logic by the words "fx is false for all values of x." The negation of this would be the proposition "there is at least one x for which fx is true" which is represented by "$(\exists x) . fx$." If we had started with not-fx instead of fx we should have arrived at the proposition "fx is true for all values of x" which is represented by "$(x) . fx$." Wittgenstein's method of dealing with general propositions [*i.e.* "$(x) . fx$" and "$(\exists x) . fx$"] differs from previous methods by the fact that the generality comes only in specifying the set of propositions concerned, and when this has been done the building up of truth-functions proceeds exactly as it would in the case of a finite number of enumerated arguments $p, q, r \ldots$.

Mr Wittgenstein's explanation of his symbolism at this point is not quite fully given in the text. The symbol he uses is $(\overline{p}, \overline{\xi}, N(\overline{\xi}))$. The following is the explanation of this symbol:

$\overline{p}$ stands for all atomic propositions.

$\overline{\xi}$ stands for any set of propositions.

$N(\overline{\xi})$ stands for the negation of all the propositions making up $\overline{\xi}$.

The whole symbol $(\overline{p}, \overline{\xi}, N(\overline{\xi}))$ means whatever can be obtained by taking any selection of atomic propositions, negating them all, then taking any selection of the set of propositions now obtained, together with any of the originals—and so on indefinitely. This is, he says, the general truth-function and also the general form of proposition. What is meant is somewhat less complicated than it sounds. The symbol is intended to describe a process by the help of which, given the atomic propositions, all others can be manufactured. The process depends upon:

(a) Sheffer's proof that all truth-functions can be obtained out of simultaneous negation, i.e. out of "not-p and not-q";

(b) Mr Wittgenstein's theory of the derivation of general propositions from conjunctions and disjunctions;

(c) The assertion that a proposition can only occur in another proposition as argument to a truth-function. Given these three foundations, it follows that all propositions which are not atomic can be derived from such as are, by a uniform process, and it is this process which is indicated by Mr Wittgenstein's symbol.

From this uniform method of construction we arrive at an amazing simplification of the theory of inference, as well as a definition of the sort of propositions that belong to logic. The method of generation which has just been described, enables Wittgenstein to say that all propositions can be constructed in the above manner from atomic propositions, and in this way the totality of propositions is defined. (The apparent exceptions which we mentioned above are dealt with in a manner which we shall consider later.) Wittgenstein is enabled to assert that propositions are all that follows from the totality of atomic propositions (together with the fact that it is the totality of them); that a proposition is always a truth-function of atomic propositions; and that if p follows from q the meaning of p is contained in the meaning of q, from which of course it results that nothing can be deduced from an atomic proposition. All the propositions of logic, he maintains, are tautologies, such, for example, as "p or not p."

The fact that nothing can be deduced from an atomic proposition has interesting applications, for example, to causality. There cannot, in Wittgenstein's logic, be any such thing as a causal nexus. "The events of the future," he says, "*cannot* be inferred from those of the present. Superstition is the belief in the causal nexus." That the sun will rise to-morrow is a hypothesis. We do not in fact know whether it will rise, since there is no compulsion according to which one thing must happen because another happens.

Let us now take up another subject—that of names. In Wittgenstein's theoretical logical language, names are only given to simples. We do not give two names to one thing, or one name to two things. There is no way whatever, according to him, by which we can describe the totality of things that can be named, in other words, the totality of what there is in the world. In order to be able to do this we should have to know of some property which must belong to every thing by a logical necessity. It has been sought to find such a property in self-identity, but the conception of identity is subjected by Wittgenstein to a destructive criticism from which there seems no escape. The definition of identity by means of the identity of indiscernibles is rejected, because the identity of indiscernibles appears to be not a logically necessary principle. According to this principle x is identical with y if every property of x is a property of y, but it would, after all, be logically possible for two things to have exactly the same properties. If this does not in fact happen that is an accidental characteristic of the world, not a logically necessary characteristic, and accidental characteristics of the world must, of course, not be admitted into the structure of logic. Mr Wittgenstein accordingly banishes identity and adopts the convention that different letters are to mean different things. In practice, identity is needed as between a name and a description or between two descriptions. It is needed for such propositions as "Socrates is the philosopher who drank the hemlock," or "The even prime is the next number after 1." For such uses of identity it is easy to provide on Wittgenstein's system.

The rejection of identity removes one method of speaking of the totality of things, and it will be found that any other method that may be suggested is equally fallacious: so, at least, Wittgenstein contends and, I think, rightly. This amounts to saying that "object" is a pseudo-concept. To say "x is an object" is to say nothing. It follows from this that we cannot make such statements as "there are more than three objects in the world," or "there are an infinite number of objects in the world." Objects can only be mentioned in connexion with some definite property. We can say "there are more than three objects which are human," or "there are more than three objects which are red," for in these statements the word object can be replaced by a variable in the language of logic, the variable being one which satisfies in the first case the function "x is human"; in the second the function "x is red." But when we attempt to say "there are more than three objects," this substitution of the variable for the word "object" becomes impossible, and the proposition is therefore seen to be meaningless.

We here touch one instance of Wittgenstein's fundamental thesis, that it is impossible to say anything about the world as a whole, and that whatever can be said has to be about bounded portions of the world. This view may have been originally suggested by notation, and if so, that is much in its favour, for a good notation has a subtlety and suggestiveness which at times make it seem almost like a live teacher. Notational irregularities are often the first sign of philosophical errors, and a perfect notation would be a substitute for thought. But although notation may have first suggested to Mr Wittgenstein the limitation of logic to things within the world as opposed to the world as a whole, yet the view, once suggested, is seen to have much else to recommend it. Whether it is ultimately true I do not, for my part, profess to know. In this Introduction I am concerned to expound it, not to pronounce upon it. According to this view we could only say things about the world as a whole if we could get outside the world, if, that is to say, it ceased to be for us the whole world. Our world may be bounded for some superior being who can survey it from above, but for us, however finite it may be, it cannot have a boundary, since it has nothing outside it. Wittgenstein uses, as an analogy, the field of vision. Our field of vision does not, for us, have a visual boundary, just because there is nothing outside it, and in like manner our logical world has no logical boundary because our logic knows of nothing outside it. These considerations lead him to a somewhat curious discussion of Solipsism. Logic, he says, fills the world. The boundaries of the world are also its boundaries. In logic, therefore, we cannot say, there is this and this in the world, but not that, for to say so would apparently presuppose that we exclude certain possibilities, and this cannot be the case, since it would require that logic should go beyond the boundaries of the world as if it could contemplate these boundaries from the other side

15

also. What we cannot think we cannot think, therefore we also cannot say what we cannot think.

This, he says, gives the key to Solipsism. What Solipsism intends is quite correct, but this cannot be said, it can only be shown. That the world is *my* world appears in the fact that the boundaries of language (the only language I understand) indicate the boundaries of my world. The metaphysical subject does not belong to the world but is a boundary of the world.

We must take up next the question of molecular propositions which are at first sight not truth-functions, of the propositions that they contain, such, for example, as "A believes *p*."

Wittgenstein introduces this subject in the statement of his position, namely, that all molecular functions are truth-functions. He says (5.54): "In the general propositional form, propositions occur in a proposition only as bases of truth-operations." At first sight, he goes on to explain, it seems as if a proposition could also occur in other ways, *e.g.* "A believes *p*." Here it seems superficially as if the proposition *p* stood in a sort of relation to the object A. "But it is clear that 'A believes that *p*,' 'A thinks *p*,' 'A says *p*' are of the form '*p* says *p*'; and here we have no co-ordination of a fact and an object, but a co-ordination of facts by means of a co-ordination of their objects" (5.542).

What Mr Wittgenstein says here is said so shortly that its point is not likely to be clear to those who have not in mind the controversies with which he is concerned. The theory with which he is disagreeing will be found in my articles on the nature of truth and falsehood in *Philosophical Essays* and *Proceedings of the Aristotelian Society*, 1906–7. The problem at issue is the problem of the logical form of belief, *i.e.* what is the schema representing what occurs when a man believes. Of course, the problem applies not only to belief, but also to a host of other mental phenomena which may be called propositional attitudes: doubting, considering, desiring, etc. In all these cases it seems natural to express the phenomenon in the form "A doubts *p*," "A desires *p*," etc., which makes it appear as though we were dealing with a relation between a person and a proposition. This cannot, of course, be the ultimate analysis, since persons are fictions and so are propositions, except in the sense in which they are facts on their own account. A proposition, considered as a fact on its own account, may be a set of words which a man says over to himself, or a complex image, or train of images passing through his mind, or a set of incipient bodily movements. It may be any one of innumerable different things. The proposition as a fact on its own account, for example the actual set of words the man pronounces to himself, is not relevant to logic. What is relevant to logic is that common element among all these facts, which enables him, as we say, to *mean* the fact which the proposition asserts. To psychology, of course, more is relevant; for a symbol does not mean what it symbolizes in virtue of a logical relation alone, but in virtue also of a psychological relation of intention, or association, or what-not. The psychological part of meaning, however, does not concern the logician. What does concern him in this problem of belief is the logical schema. It is clear that, when a person believes a proposition, the person, considered as a metaphysical subject, does not have to be assumed in order to explain what is happening. What has to be explained is the relation between the set of words which is the proposition considered as a fact on its own account, and the "objective" fact which makes the proposition true or false. This reduces ultimately to the question of the meaning of propositions, that is to say, the meaning of propositions is the only non-psychological portion of the problem involved in the analysis of belief. This problem is simply one of a relation of two facts, namely, the relation between the series of words used by the believer and the fact which makes these words true or false. The series of words is a fact just as much as what makes it true or false is a fact. The relation between these two facts is not unanalysable, since the meaning of a proposition results from the meaning of its constituent words. The meaning of the series of words which is a proposition is a function of the meanings of the separate words. Accordingly, the proposition as a whole does not really enter into what has to be explained in explaining the meaning of a proposition. It would perhaps help to suggest the point of view which I am trying to indicate, to say that in the cases we have been considering the proposition occurs as a fact, not as a proposition. Such a statement, however, must not be taken too literally. The real point is that in believing, desiring, etc., what is logically fundamental is the relation of a proposition *considered as a fact*, to the fact which makes it true or false, and that this relation of two facts is reducible to a relation of their constituents. Thus the proposition does not occur at all in the same sense in which it occurs in a truth-function.

There are some respects, in which, as it seems to me, Mr Wittgenstein's theory stands in need of greater technical development. This applies in particular to his theory of number (6.02 ff.) which, as it stands, is only capable of dealing with finite numbers. No logic can be considered adequate until it has been shown to be capable of dealing with transfinite numbers. I do not think there is anything in Mr Wittgenstein's system to make it impossible for him to fill this lacuna. More interesting than such questions of comparative detail is Mr Wittgenstein's attitude towards the mystical. His attitude upon this grows naturally out of his doctrine in pure logic, according to which the logical proposition is a picture (true or false) of the fact, and has in common with the fact a certain structure. It is this common structure which makes it capable of being a picture of the fact, but the structure cannot itself be put into words, since it is a structure *of* words, as well as of the facts to which they refer. Everything, therefore, which is involved in the very idea of the expressiveness of language must remain incapable of being expressed in language, and is, therefore, inexpressible in a perfectly precise sense. This inexpressible contains, according to Mr Wittgenstein, the whole of logic and philosophy. The right method of teaching philosophy, he says, would be to confine oneself to propositions of the sciences, stated with all possible clearness and exactness, leaving philosophical assertions to the learner, and proving to him, whenever he made them, that they are meaningless. It is true that the fate of Socrates might befall a man who attempted this method of teaching, but we are not to be deterred by that fear, if it is the only right method. It is not this that causes some hesitation in accepting Mr Wittgenstein's position, in spite of the very powerful arguments which he brings to its support. What causes hesitation is the fact that, after all, Mr Wittgenstein manages to say a good deal about what cannot be said, thus suggesting to the sceptical reader that possibly there may be some loophole through a hierarchy of languages, or by some other exit. The whole subject of ethics, for example, is placed by Mr Wittgenstein in the mystical, inexpressible region. Nevertheless he is capable of conveying his ethical opinions. His defence would be that what he calls the mystical can be shown, although it cannot be said. It may be that this defence is adequate, but, for my part, I confess that it leaves me with a certain sense of intellectual discomfort.

There is one purely logical problem in regard to which these difficulties are peculiarly acute. I mean the problem of generality. In the theory of generality it is necessary to consider all propositions of the form fx where fx is a given propositional function. This belongs to the part of logic which can be expressed, according to Mr Wittgenstein's system. But the totality of possible values of x which might seem to be involved in the totality of propositions of the form fx is not admitted by Mr Wittgenstein among the things that can be spoken of, for this is no other than the totality of things in the world, and thus involves the attempt to conceive the world as a whole; "the feeling of the world as a bounded whole is the mystical"; hence the totality of the values of x is mystical (6.45). This is expressly argued when Mr Wittgenstein denies that we can make propositions as to how many things there are in the world, as for example, that there are more than three.

These difficulties suggest to my mind some such possibility as this: that every language has, as Mr Wittgenstein says, a structure concerning which, *in the language*, nothing can be said, but that there may be another language dealing with the structure of the first language, and having itself a new structure, and that to this hierarchy of languages there may be no limit. Mr Wittgenstein would of course reply that his whole theory is applicable unchanged to the totality of such languages. The only retort would be to deny that there is any such totality. The totalities concerning which Mr Wittgenstein holds that it is impossible to speak logically are nevertheless thought by him to exist, and are the subject-matter of his mysticism. The totality resulting from our hierarchy would be not merely logically inexpressible, but a fiction, a mere delusion, and in this way the supposed sphere of the mystical would be abolished. Such an hypothesis is very difficult, and I can see objections to it which at the moment I do not know how to answer. Yet I do not see how any easier hypothesis can escape from Mr Wittgenstein's conclusions. Even if this very difficult hypothesis should prove tenable, it would leave untouched a very large part of Mr Wittgenstein's theory, though possibly not the part upon which he himself would wish to lay most stress. As one with a long experience of the difficulties of logic and of the deceptiveness of theories which seem irrefutable, I find myself unable to be sure of the rightness of a theory, merely on the ground that I cannot see any point on which it is wrong. But to have constructed a theory of logic which is not at any point obviously wrong is to have achieved a work of extraordinary difficulty and importance. This merit, in my opinion, belongs to Mr Wittgenstein's book, and makes it one which no serious philosopher can afford to neglect.

BERTRAND RUSSELL.

May 1922.

Tractatus Logico-Philosophicus

DEDICATED
TO THE MEMORY OF MY FRIEND
DAVID H. PINSENT

Motto: ... und alles, was man weiss, nicht bloss rauschen
und brausen gehört hat, lässt sich in drei Worten sagen.

KÜRNBERGER.

Tractatus Logico-Philosophicus

PREFACE

This book will perhaps only be understood by those who have themselves already thought the thoughts which are expressed in it—or similar thoughts. It is therefore not a text-book. Its object would be attained if there were one person who read it with understanding and to whom it afforded pleasure.

The book deals with the problems of philosophy and shows, as I believe, that the method of formulating these problems rests on the misunderstanding of the logic of our language. Its whole meaning could be summed up somewhat as follows: What can be said at all can be said clearly; and whereof one cannot speak thereof one must be silent.

The book will, therefore, draw a limit to thinking, or rather—not to thinking, but to the expression of thoughts; for, in order to draw a limit to thinking we should have to be able to think both sides of this limit (we should therefore have to be able to think what cannot be thought).

The limit can, therefore, only be drawn in language and what lies on the other side of the limit will be simply nonsense.

How far my efforts agree with those of other philosophers I will not decide. Indeed what I have here written makes no claim to novelty in points of detail; and therefore I give no sources, because it is indifferent to me whether what I have thought has already been thought before me by another.

I will only mention that to the great works of Frege and the writings of my friend Bertrand Russell I owe in large measure the stimulation of my thoughts.

If this work has a value it consists in two things. First that in it thoughts are expressed, and this value will be the greater the better the thoughts are expressed. The more the nail has been hit on the head.— Here I am conscious that I have fallen far short of the possible. Simply because my powers are insufficient to cope with the task.—May others come and do it better.

On the other hand the *truth* of the thoughts communicated here seems to me unassailable and definitive. I am, therefore, of the opinion that the problems have in essentials been finally solved. And if I am not mistaken in this, then the value of this work secondly consists in the fact that it shows how little has been done when these problems have been solved.

1	The world is everything that is the case.*
1.1	The world is the totality of facts, not of things.
1.11	The world is determined by the facts, and by these being *all* the facts.
1.12	For the totality of facts determines both what is the case, and also all that is not the case.
1.13	The facts in logical space are the world.
1.2	The world divides into facts.
1.21	Any one can either be the case or not be the case, and everything else remain the same.
2	What is the case, the fact, is the existence of atomic facts.
2.01	An atomic fact is a combination of objects (entities, things).
2.011	It is essential to a thing that it can be a constituent part of an atomic fact.
2.012	In logic nothing is accidental: if a thing *can* occur in an atomic fact the possibility of that atomic fact must already be prejudged in the thing.
2.0121	It would, so to speak, appear as an accident, when to a thing that could exist alone on its own account, subsequently a state of affairs could be made to fit.
	If things can occur in atomic facts, this possibility must already lie in them.

*The decimal figures as numbers of the separate propositions indicate the logical importance of the propositions, the emphasis laid upon them in my exposition. The propositions *n*.1, *n*.2, *n*.3, etc., are comments on proposition No. *n*; the propositions *n.m*1, *n.m*2, etc., are comments on the proposition No. *n.m*; and so on.

(A logical entity cannot be merely possible. Logic treats of every possibility, and all possibilities are its facts.)

Just as we cannot think of spatial objects at all apart from space, or temporal objects apart from time, so we cannot think of *any* object apart from the possibility of its connexion with other things.

If I can think of an object in the context of an atomic fact, I cannot think of it apart from the *possibility* of this context.

2.0122 The thing is independent, in so far as it can occur in all *possible* circumstances, but this form of independence is a form of connexion with the atomic fact, a form of dependence. (It is impossible for words to occur in two different ways, alone and in the proposition.)

2.0123 If I know an object, then I also know all the possibilities of its occurrence in atomic facts.

(Every such possibility must lie in the nature of the object.)

A new possibility cannot subsequently be found.

2.01231 In order to know an object, I must know not its external but all its internal qualities.

2.0124 If all objects are given, then thereby are all *possible* atomic facts also given.

2.013 Every thing is, as it were, in a space of possible atomic facts. I can think of this space as empty, but not of the thing without the space.

2.0131 A spatial object must lie in infinite space. (A point in space is a place for an argument.)

A speck in a visual field need not be red, but it must have a colour; it has, so to speak, a colour space round it. A tone must have *a* pitch, the object of the sense of touch *a* hardness, etc.

2.014 Objects contain the possibility of all states of affairs.

2.0141 The possibility of its occurrence in atomic facts is the form of the object.

2.02 The object is simple.

2.0201 Every statement about complexes can be analysed into a statement about their constituent parts, and into those propositions which completely describe the complexes.

2.021 Objects form the substance of the world. Therefore they cannot be compound.

2.0211 If the world had no substance, then whether a proposition had sense would depend on whether another proposition was true.

2.0212 It would then be impossible to form a picture of the world (true or false).

2.022 It is clear that however different from the real one an imagined world may be, it must have something—a form—in common with the real world.

2.023 This fixed form consists of the objects.

2.0231 The substance of the world *can* only determine a form and not any material properties. For these are first presented by the propositions—first formed by the configuration of the objects.

2.0232 Roughly speaking: objects are colourless.

2.0233 Two objects of the same logical form are—apart from their external properties—only differentiated from one another in that they are different.

2.02331 Either a thing has properties which no other has, and then one can distinguish it straight away from the others by a description and refer to it; or, on the other hand, there are several things which have the totality of their properties in common, and then it is quite impossible to point to any one of them.

For if a thing is not distinguished by anything, I cannot distinguish it—for otherwise it would be distinguished.

2.024 Substance is what exists independently of what is the case.

2.025 It is form and content.

2.0251 Space, time and colour (colouredness) are forms of objects.

2.026 Only if there are objects can there be a fixed form of the world.

2.027 The fixed, the existent and the object are one.

2.0271 The object is the fixed, the existent; the configuration is the changing, the variable.

2.0272   The configuration of the objects forms the atomic fact.

2.03   In the atomic fact objects hang one in another, like the members of a chain.

2.031   In the atomic fact the objects are combined in a definite way.

2.032   The way in which objects hang together in the atomic fact is the structure of the atomic fact.

2.033   The form is the possibility of the structure.

2.034   The structure of the fact consists of the structures of the atomic facts.

2.04   The totality of existent atomic facts is the world.

2.05   The totality of existent atomic facts also determines which atomic facts do not exist.

2.06   The existence and non-existence of atomic facts is the reality.
       (The existence of atomic facts we also call a positive fact, their non-existence a negative fact.)

2.061   Atomic facts are independent of one another.

2.062   From the existence or non-existence of an atomic fact we cannot infer the existence or non-existence of another.

2.063   The total reality is the world.

2.1   We make to ourselves pictures of facts.

2.11   The picture presents the facts in logical space, the existence and non-existence of atomic facts.

2.12   The picture is a model of reality.

2.13   To the objects correspond in the picture the elements of the picture.

2.131   The elements of the picture stand, in the picture, for the objects.

2.14   The picture consists in the fact that its elements are combined with one another in a definite way.

2.141   The picture is a fact.

2.15   That the elements of the picture are combined with one another in a definite way, represents that the things are so combined with one another.

This connexion of the elements of the picture is called its structure, and the possibility of this structure is called the form of representation of the picture.

2.151 The form of representation is the possibility that the things are combined with one another as are the elements of the picture.

2.1511 Thus the picture is linked with reality; it reaches up to it.

2.1512 It is like a scale applied to reality.

2.15121 Only the outermost points of the dividing lines *touch* the object to be measured.

2.1513 According to this view the representing relation which makes it a picture, also belongs to the picture.

2.1514 The representing relation consists of the co-ordinations of the elements of the picture and the things.

2.1515 These co-ordinations are as it were the feelers of its elements with which the picture touches reality.

2.16 In order to be a picture a fact must have something in common with what it pictures.

2.161 In the picture and the pictured there must be something identical in order that the one can be a picture of the other at all.

2.17 What the picture must have in common with reality in order to be able to represent it after its manner—rightly or falsely—is its form of representation.

2.171 The picture can represent every reality whose form it has.

The spatial picture, everything spatial, the coloured, everything coloured, etc.

2.172 The picture, however, cannot represent its form of representation; it shows it forth.

2.173 The picture represents its object from without (its standpoint is its form of representation), therefore the picture represents its object rightly or falsely.

2.174 But the picture cannot place itself outside of its form of representation.

2.18 What every picture, of whatever form, must have in common with reality in order to be able to represent it at all—rightly or falsely—is the logical form, that is, the form of reality.

2.181   If the form of representation is the logical form, then the picture is called a logical picture.

2.182   Every picture is *also* a logical picture. (On the other hand, for example, not every picture is spatial.)

2.19   The logical picture can depict the world.

2.2   The picture has the logical form of representation in common with what it pictures.

2.201   The picture depicts reality by representing a possibility of the existence and non-existence of atomic facts.

2.202   The picture represents a possible state of affairs in logical space.

2.203   The picture contains the possibility of the state of affairs which it represents.

2.21   The picture agrees with reality or not; it is right or wrong, true or false.

2.22   The picture represents what it represents, independently of its truth or falsehood, through the form of representation.

2.221   What the picture represents is its sense.

2.222   In the agreement or disagreement of its sense with reality, its truth or falsity consists.

2.223   In order to discover whether the picture is true or false we must compare it with reality.

2.224   It cannot be discovered from the picture alone whether it is true or false.

2.225   There is no picture which is a priori true.

3   The logical picture of the facts is the thought.

3.001   "An atomic fact is thinkable"—means: we can imagine it.

3.01   The totality of true thoughts is a picture of the world.

3.02   The thought contains the possibility of the state of affairs which it thinks.
What is thinkable is also possible.

3.03   We cannot think anything unlogical, for otherwise we should have to think unlogically.

3.031   It used to be said that God could create everything, except what was contrary to the laws of logic. The truth is, we could not *say* of an "unlogical" world how it would look.

3.032   To present in language anything which "contradicts logic" is as impossible as in geometry to present by its co-ordinates a figure which contradicts the laws of space; or to give the co-ordinates of a point which does not exist.

3.0321 We could present spatially an atomic fact which contradicted the laws of physics, but not one which contradicted the laws of geometry.

3.04   An a priori true thought would be one whose possibility guaranteed its truth.

3.05   We could only know a priori that a thought is true if its truth was to be recognized from the thought itself (without an object of comparison).

3.1   In the proposition the thought is expressed perceptibly through the senses.

3.11   We use the sensibly perceptible sign (sound or written sign, etc.) of the proposition as a projection of the possible state of affairs.

        The method of projection is the thinking of the sense of the proposition.

3.12   The sign through which we express the thought I call the propositional sign. And the proposition is the propositional sign in its projective relation to the world.

3.13   To the proposition belongs everything which belongs to the projection; but not what is projected.

        Therefore the possibility of what is projected but not this itself.

        In the proposition, therefore, its sense is not yet contained, but the possibility of expressing it.

        ("The content of the proposition" means the content of the significant proposition.)

        In the proposition the form of its sense is contained, but not its content.

31

3.14   The propositional sign consists in the fact that its elements, the words, are combined in it in a definite way.

The propositional sign is a fact.

3.141   The proposition is not a mixture of words (just as the musical theme is not a mixture of tones).

The proposition is articulate.

3.142   Only facts can express a sense, a class of names cannot.

3.143   That the propositional sign is a fact is concealed by the ordinary form of expression, written or printed.

(For in the printed proposition, for example, the sign of a proposition does not appear essentially different from a word. Thus it was possible for Frege to call the proposition a compounded name.)

3.1431   The essential nature of the propositional sign becomes very clear when we imagine it made up of spatial objects (such as tables, chairs, books) instead of written signs.

The mutual spatial position of these things then expresses the sense of the proposition.

3.1432   We must not say, "The complex sign 'aRb' says 'a stands in relation R to b'"; but we must say, "*That* 'a' stands in a certain relation to 'b' says *that aRb*".

3.144   States of affairs can be described but not *named*.

(Names resemble points; propositions resemble arrows, they have sense.)

3.2   In propositions thoughts can be so expressed that to the objects of the thoughts correspond the elements of the propositional sign.

3.201   These elements I call "simple signs" and the proposition "completely analysed".

3.202   The simple signs employed in propositions are called names.

3.203   The name means the object. The object is its meaning. ("A" is the same sign as "A".)

3.21   To the configuration of the simple signs in the propositional sign corresponds the configuration of the objects in the state of affairs.

3.22   In the proposition the name represents the object.

3.221   Objects I can only *name*. Signs represent them. I can only speak *of* them. I cannot *assert them*. A proposition can only say *how* a thing is, not *what* it is.

3.23   The postulate of the possibility of the simple signs is the postulate of the determinateness of the sense.

3.24   A proposition about a complex stands in internal relation to the proposition about its constituent part.

A complex can only be given by its description, and this will either be right or wrong. The proposition in which there is mention of a complex, if this does not exist, becomes not nonsense but simply false.

That a propositional element signifies a complex can be seen from an indeterminateness in the propositions in which it occurs. We *know* that everything is not yet determined by this proposition. (The notation for generality *contains* a prototype.)

The combination of the symbols of a complex in a simple symbol can be expressed by a definition.

3.25   There is one and only one complete analysis of the proposition.

3.251   The proposition expresses what it expresses in a definite and clearly specifiable way: the proposition is articulate.

3.26   The name cannot be analysed further by any definition. It is a primitive sign.

3.261   Every defined sign signifies *via* those signs by which it is defined, and the definitions show the way.

Two signs, one a primitive sign, and one defined by primitive signs, cannot signify in the same way. Names *cannot* be taken to pieces by definition (nor any sign which alone and independently has a meaning).

3.262   What does not get expressed in the sign is shown by its application. What the signs conceal, their application declares.

3.263   The meanings of primitive signs can be explained by elucidations. Elucidations are propositions which contain the primitive signs. They can, therefore, only be understood when the meanings of these signs are already known.

3.3   Only the proposition has sense; only in the context of a proposition has a name meaning.

3.31   Every part of a proposition which characterizes its sense I call an expression (a symbol).

(The proposition itself is an expression.)

Expressions are everything—essential for the sense of the proposition—that propositions can have in common with one another

An expression characterizes a form and a content.

3.311   An expression presupposes the forms of all propositions in which it can occur. It is the common characteristic mark of a class of propositions.

3.312   It is therefore represented by the general form of the propositions which it characterizes.

And in this form the expression is *constant* and everything else *variable*.

3.313   An expression is thus presented by a variable, whose values are the propositions which contain the expression.

(In the limiting case the variables become constants, the expression a proposition.)

I call such a variable a "propositional variable".

3.314   An expression has meaning only in a proposition. Every variable can be conceived as a propositional variable.

(Including the variable name.)

3.315   If we change a constituent part of a proposition into a variable, there is a class of propositions which are all the values of the resulting variable proposition. This class in general still depends on what, by arbitrary agreement, we mean by parts of that proposition. But if we change all those signs, whose meaning was arbitrarily determined, into variables, there always remains such a class. But this is now no longer dependent on any agreement; it depends only on the nature of the proposition. It corresponds to a logical form, to a logical prototype.

3.316   What values the propositional variable can assume is determined.

The determination of the values *is* the variable.

3.317 The determination of the values of the propositional variable is done by *indicating the propositions* whose common mark the variable is.

The determination is a description of these propositions.

The determination will therefore deal only with symbols not with their meaning.

And *only* this is essential to the determination, *that it is only a description of symbols and asserts nothing about what is symbolized.*

The way in which we describe the propositions is not essential.

3.318 I conceive the proposition—like Frege and Russell—as a function of the expressions contained in it.

3.32 The sign is the part of the symbol perceptible by the senses.

3.321 Two different symbols can therefore have the sign (the written sign or the sound sign) in common—they then signify in different ways.

3.322 It can never indicate the common characteristic of two objects that we symbolize them with the same signs but by different *methods of symbolizing.* For the sign is arbitrary. We could therefore equally well choose two different signs and where then would be what was common in the symbolization.

3.323 In the language of everyday life it very often happens that the same word signifies in two different ways—and therefore belongs to two different symbols—or that two words, which signify in different ways, are apparently applied in the same way in the proposition.

Thus the word "is" appears as the copula, as the sign of equality, and as the expression of existence; "to exist" as an intransitive verb like "to go"; "identical" as an adjective; we speak of *something* but also of the fact of *something* happening.

(In the proposition "Green is green"—where the first word is a proper name and the last an adjective—these words have not merely different meanings but they are *different symbols.*)

35

3.324　Thus there easily arise the most fundamental confusions (of which the whole of philosophy is full).

3.325　In order to avoid these errors, we must employ a symbolism which excludes them, by not applying the same sign in different symbols and by not applying signs in the same way which signify in different ways. A symbolism, that is to say, which obeys the rules of *logical* grammar—of logical syntax.

(The logical symbolism of Frege and Russell is such a language, which, however, does still not exclude all errors.)

3.326　In order to recognize the symbol in the sign we must consider the significant use.

3.327　The sign determines a logical form only together with its logical syntactic application.

3.328　If a sign is *not necessary* then it is meaningless. That is the meaning of Occam's razor.

(If everything in the symbolism works as though a sign had meaning, then it has meaning.)

3.33　In logical syntax the meaning of a sign ought never to play a rôle; it must admit of being established without mention being thereby made of the *meaning* of a sign; it ought to presuppose *only* the description of the expressions.

3.331　From this observation we get a further view—into Russell's *Theory of Types*. Russell's error is shown by the fact that in drawing up his symbolic rules he has to speak of the meaning of the signs.

3.332　No proposition can say anything about itself, because the propositional sign cannot be contained in itself (that is the "whole theory of types").

3.333　A function cannot be its own argument, because the functional sign already contains the prototype of its own argument and it cannot contain itself.

If, for example, we suppose that the function $F(fx)$ could be its own argument, then there would be a proposition "$F(F(fx))$", and in this the outer function F and the inner function F must have different meanings; for the inner has the form $\phi(fx)$, the outer the form $\psi(\phi(fx))$. Common to both functions is only the letter "F", which by itself signifies nothing. This is at once clear, if instead of "$F(F(u))$" we write "$(\exists\phi) : F(\phi u) . \phi u = Fu$". Herewith Russell's paradox vanishes.

3.334 The rules of logical syntax must follow of themselves, if we only know how every single sign signifies.

3.34 A proposition possesses essential and accidental features. Accidental are the features which are due to a particular way of producing the propositional sign. Essential are those which alone enable the proposition to express its sense.

3.341 The essential in a proposition is therefore that which is common to all propositions which can express the same sense.

And in the same way in general the essential in a symbol is that which all symbols which can fulfil the same purpose have in common.

3.3411 One could therefore say the real name is that which all symbols, which signify an object, have in common. It would then follow, step by step, that no sort of composition was essential for a name.

3.342 In our notations there is indeed something arbitrary, but *this* is not arbitrary, namely that *if* we have determined anything arbitrarily, then something else *must* be the case. (This results from the *essence* of the notation.)

3.3421 A particular method of symbolizing may be unimportant, but it is always important that this is a *possible* method of symbolizing. And this happens as a rule in philosophy: The single thing proves over and over again to be unimportant, but the possibility of every single thing reveals something about the nature of the world.

3.343 Definitions are rules for the translation of one language into another. Every correct symbolism must be translatable into every other according to such rules. It is *this* which all have in common.

3.344   What signifies in the symbol is what is common to all those symbols by which it can be replaced according to the rules of logical syntax.

3.3441   We can, for example, express what is common to all notations for the truth-functions as follows: It is common to them that they all, for example, *can be replaced* by the notations of "$\sim p$" ("not p") and "$p \vee q$" ("p or q").

      (Herewith is indicated the way in which a special possible notation can give us general information.)

3.3442   The sign of the complex is not arbitrarily resolved in the analysis, in such a way that its resolution would be different in every propositional structure.

3.4   The proposition determines a place in logical space: the existence of this logical place is guaranteed by the existence of the constituent parts alone, by the existence of the significant proposition.

3.41   The propositional sign and the logical co-ordinates: that is the logical place.

3.411   The geometrical and the logical place agree in that each is the possibility of an existence.

3.42   Although a proposition may only determine one place in logical space, the whole logical space must already be given by it.

      (Otherwise denial, the logical sum, the logical product, etc., would always introduce new elements—in co-ordination.)

      (The logical scaffolding round the picture determines the logical space. The proposition reaches through the whole logical space.)

3.5   The applied, thought, propositional sign is the thought.

4   The thought is the significant proposition.

4.001   The totality of propositions is the language.

4.002   Man possesses the capacity of constructing languages, in which every sense can be expressed, without having an idea how and what each word means—just as one speaks without knowing how the single sounds are produced.

Colloquial language is a part of the human organism and is not less complicated than it.
From it it is humanly impossible to gather immediately the logic of language.
Language disguises the thought; so that from the external form of the clothes one cannot infer the form of the thought they clothe, because the external form of the clothes is constructed with quite another object than to let the form of the body be recognized.
The silent adjustments to understand colloquial language are enormously complicated.

4.003   Most propositions and questions, that have been written about philosophical matters, are not false, but senseless. We cannot, therefore, answer questions of this kind at all, but only state their senselessness. Most questions and propositions of the philosophers result from the fact that we do not understand the logic of our language.

(They are of the same kind as the question whether the Good is more or less identical than the Beautiful.)

And so it is not to be wondered at that the deepest problems are really *no* problems.

4.0031   All philosophy is "Critique of language" (but not at all in Mauthner's sense). Russell's merit is to have shown that the apparent logical form of the proposition need not be its real form.

4.01   The proposition is a picture of reality.

The proposition is a model of the reality as we think it is.

4.011   At the first glance the proposition—say as it stands printed on paper—does not seem to be a picture of the reality of which it treats. But nor does the musical score appear at first sight to be a picture of a musical piece; nor does our phonetic spelling (letters) seem to be a picture of our spoken language. And yet these symbolisms prove to be pictures—even in the ordinary sense of the word—of what they represent.

4.012   It is obvious that we perceive a proposition of the form aRb as a picture. Here the sign is obviously a likeness of the signified.

4.013   And if we penetrate to the essence of this pictorial nature we see that this is not disturbed by *apparent irregularities* (like the use of ♯ and ♭ in the score).

For these irregularities also picture what they are to express; only in another way.

4.014 The gramophone record, the musical thought, the score, the waves of sound, all stand to one another in that pictorial internal relation, which holds between language and the world. To all of them the logical structure is common.

(Like the two youths, their two horses and their lilies in the story. They are all in a certain sense one.)

4.0141 In the fact that there is a general rule by which the musician is able to read the symphony out of the score, and that there is a rule by which one could reconstruct the symphony from the line on a gramophone record and from this again—by means of the first rule—construct the score, herein lies the internal similarity between these things which at first sight seem to be entirely different. And the rule is the law of projection which projects the symphony into the language of the musical score. It is the rule of translation of this language into the language of the gramophone record.

4.015 The possibility of all similes, of all the imagery of our language, rests on the logic of representation.

4.016 In order to understand the essence of the proposition, consider hieroglyphic writing, which pictures the facts it describes.

And from it came the alphabet without the essence of the representation being lost.

4.02 This we see from the fact that we understand the sense of the propositional sign, without having had it explained to us.

4.021 The proposition is a picture of reality, for I know the state of affairs presented by it, if I understand the proposition. And I understand the proposition, without its sense having been explained to me.

4.022 The proposition *shows* its sense.

The proposition *shows* how things stand, *if* it is true. And it *says*, that they do so stand.

4.023   The proposition determines reality to this extent, that one only needs to say "Yes" or "No" to it to make it agree with reality.

It must therefore be completely described by the proposition.

A proposition is the description of a fact.

As the description of an object describes it by its external properties so propositions describe reality by its internal properties.

The proposition constructs a world with the help of a logical scaffolding, and therefore one can actually see in the proposition all the logical features possessed by reality if it is true. One can *draw conclusions* from a false proposition.

4.024   To understand a proposition means to know what is the case, if it is true.

(One can therefore understand it without knowing whether it is true or not.)

One understands it if one understands its constituent parts.

4.025   The translation of one language into another is not a process of translating each proposition of the one into a proposition of the other, but only the constituent parts of propositions are translated.

(And the dictionary does not only translate substantives but also adverbs and conjunctions, etc., and it treats them all alike.)

4.026   The meanings of the simple signs (the words) must be explained to us, if we are to understand them.

By means of propositions we explain ourselves.

4.027   It is essential to propositions, that they can communicate a *new* sense to us.

4.03   A proposition must communicate a new sense with old words.

The proposition communicates to us a state of affairs, therefore it must be *essentially* connected with the state of affairs.

And the connexion is, in fact, that it is its logical picture.

The proposition only asserts something, in so far as it is a picture.

4.031   In the proposition a state of affairs is, as it were, put together for the sake of experiment.

One can say, instead of, This proposition has such and such a sense, This proposition represents such and such a state of affairs.

4.0311 One name stands for one thing, and another for another thing, and they are connected together. And so the whole, like a living picture, presents the atomic fact.

4.0312 The possibility of propositions is based upon the principle of the representation of objects by signs.

My fundamental thought is that the "logical constants" do not represent. That the *logic* of the facts cannot be represented.

4.032 The proposition is a picture of its state of affairs, only in so far as it is logically articulated.

(Even the proposition "ambulo" is composite, for its stem gives a different sense with another termination, or its termination with another stem.)

4.04 In the proposition there must be exactly as many things distinguishable as there are in the state of affairs, which it represents.

They must both possess the same logical (mathematical) multiplicity (cf. Hertz's Mechanics, on Dynamic Models).

4.041 This mathematical multiplicity naturally cannot in its turn be represented. One cannot get outside it in the representation.

4.0411 If we tried, for example, to express what is expressed by "$(x).fx$" by putting an index before fx, like: "Gen. fx", it would not do, we should not know what was generalized. If we tried to show it by an index g, like: "$f(x_g)$" it would not do—we should not know the scope of the generalization.

If we were to try it by introducing a mark in the argument places, like "$(G, G) . F(G, G)$", it would not do—we could not determine the identity of the variables, etc.

All these ways of symbolizing are inadequate because they have not the necessary mathematical multiplicity.

4.0412 For the same reason the idealist explanation of the seeing of spatial relations through "spatial spectacles" does not do, because it cannot explain the multiplicity of these relations.

4.05 Reality is compared with the proposition.

4.06 Propositions can be true or false only by being pictures of the reality.

4.061 If one does not observe that propositions have a sense independent of the facts, one can easily believe that true and false are two relations between signs and things signified with equal rights.

One could then, for example, say that "p" signifies in the true way what "$\sim p$" signifies in the false way, etc.

4.062 Can we not make ourselves understood by means of false propositions as hitherto with true ones, so long as we know that they are meant to be false? No! For a proposition is true, if what we assert by means of it is the case; and if by "p" we mean $\sim p$, and what we mean is the case, then "p" in the new conception is true and not false.

4.0621 That, however, the signs "p" and "$\sim p$" *can* say the same thing is important, for it shows that the sign "$\sim$" corresponds to nothing in reality.

That negation occurs in a proposition, is no characteristic of its sense ($\sim\sim p = p$).

The propositions "p" and "$\sim p$" have opposite senses, but to them corresponds one and the same reality.

4.063 An illustration to explain the concept of truth. A black spot on white paper; the form of the spot can be described by saying of each point of the plane whether it is white or black. To the fact that a point is black corresponds a positive fact; to the fact that a point is white (not black), a negative fact. If I indicate a point of the plane (a truth-value in Frege's terminology), this corresponds to the assumption proposed for judgment, etc. etc.

But to be able to say that a point is black or white, I must first know under what conditions a point is called white or black; in order to be able to say "p" is true (or false) I must have determined under what conditions I call "p" true, and thereby I determine the sense of the proposition.

The point at which the simile breaks down is this: we can indicate a point on the paper, without knowing what white and black are; but to a proposition without a sense corresponds nothing at all, for it signifies no thing (truth-value) whose properties are called "false" or "true"; the verb of the proposition is not "is true" or "is false"—as Frege thought—but that which "is true" must already contain the verb.

4.064 Every proposition must *already* have a sense; assertion cannot give it a sense, for what it asserts is the sense itself. And the same holds of denial, etc.

4.0641 One could say, the denial is already related to the logical place determined by the proposition that is denied.

The denying proposition determines a logical place *other* than does the proposition denied.

The denying proposition determines a logical place, with the help of the logical place of the proposition denied, by saying that it lies outside the latter place.

That one can deny again the denied proposition, shows that what is denied is already a proposition and not merely the preliminary to a proposition.

4.1 A proposition presents the existence and non-existence of atomic facts.

4.11 The totality of true propositions is the total natural science (or the totality of the natural sciences).

4.111 Philosophy is not one of the natural sciences.

(The word "philosophy" must mean something which stands above or below, but not beside the natural sciences.)

4.112 The object of philosophy is the logical clarification of thoughts.

Philosophy is not a theory but an activity.

A philosophical work consists essentially of elucidations.

The result of philosophy is not a number of "philosophical propositions", but to make propositions clear.

Philosophy should make clear and delimit sharply the thoughts which otherwise are, as it were, opaque and blurred.

4.1121 Psychology is no nearer related to philosophy, than is any other natural science.

The theory of knowledge is the philosophy of psychology.

Does not my study of sign-language correspond to the study of thought processes which philosophers held to be so essential to the philosophy of logic? Only they got entangled for the most part in unessential psychological investigations, and there is an analogous danger for my method.

4.1122 The Darwinian theory has no more to do with philosophy than has any other hypothesis of natural science.

4.113 Philosophy limits the disputable sphere of natural science.

4.114 It should limit the thinkable and thereby the unthinkable.

It should limit the unthinkable from within through the thinkable.

4.115 It will mean the unspeakable by clearly displaying the speakable.

4.116 Everything that can be thought at all can be thought clearly. Everything that can be said can be said clearly.

4.12 Propositions can represent the whole reality, but they cannot represent what they must have in common with reality in order to be able to represent it—the logical form.

To be able to represent the logical form, we should have to be able to put ourselves with the propositions outside logic, that is outside the world.

4.121 Propositions cannot represent the logical form: this mirrors itself in the propositions.

That which mirrors itself in language, language cannot represent.

That which expresses *itself* in language, *we* cannot express by language.

The propositions *show* the logical form of reality.

They exhibit it.

4.1211 Thus a proposition "*fa*" shows that in its sense the object *a* occurs, two propositions "*fa*" and "*ga*" that they are both about the same object.

If two propositions contradict one another, this is shown by their structure; similarly if one follows from another, etc.

4.1212 What *can* be shown *cannot* be said.

4.1213 Now we understand our feeling that we are in possession of the right logical conception, if only all is right in our symbolism.

4.122   We can speak in a certain sense of formal properties of objects and atomic facts, or of properties of the structure of facts, and in the same sense of formal relations and relations of structures.

(Instead of property of the structure I also say "internal property"; instead of relation of structures "internal relation".

I introduce these expressions in order to show the reason for the confusion, very widespread among philosophers, between internal relations and proper (external) relations.)

The holding of such internal properties and relations cannot, however, be asserted by propositions, but it shows itself in the propositions, which present the atomic facts and treat of the objects in question.

4.1221   An internal property of a fact we also call a feature of this fact. (In the sense in which we speak of facial features.)

4.123   A property is internal if it is unthinkable that its object does not possess it.

(This blue colour and that stand in the internal relation of brighter and darker eo ipso. It is unthinkable that *these* two objects should not stand in this relation.)

(Here to the shifting use of the words "property" and "relation" there corresponds the shifting use of the word "object".)

4.124   The existence of an internal property of a possible state of affairs is not expressed by a proposition, but it expresses itself in the proposition which presents that state of affairs, by an internal property of this proposition.

It would be as senseless to ascribe a formal property to a proposition as to deny it the formal property.

4.1241   One cannot distinguish forms from one another by saying that one has this property but the other that: for this assumes that there is a sense in asserting either property of either form.

4.125   The existence of an internal relation between possible states of affairs expresses itself in language by an internal relation between the propositions presenting them.

4.1251   Here the disputed question "whether all relations are internal or external" disappears.

4.1252 Series which are ordered by *internal* relations I call formal series. The series of numbers is ordered not by an external, but by an internal relation.

Similarly the series of propositions "aRb",

"$(\exists x) : aRx . xRb$",

"$(\exists x, y) : aRx . aRy . yRb$", etc.

(If b stands in one of these relations to a, I call b a successor of a.)

4.126 In the sense in which we speak of formal properties we can now speak also of formal concepts.

(I introduce this expression in order to make clear the confusion of formal concepts with proper concepts which runs through the whole of the old logic.)

That anything falls under a formal concept as an object belonging to it, cannot be expressed by a proposition. But it shows itself in the sign of this object itself. (The name shows that it signifies an object, the numerical sign that it signifies a number, etc.)

Formal concepts cannot, like proper concepts, be presented by a function.

For their characteristics, the formal properties, are not expressed by the functions.

The expression of a formal property is a feature of certain symbols.

The sign that signifies the characteristics of a formal concept is, therefore, a characteristic feature of all symbols, whose meanings fall under the concept.

The expression of the formal concept is therefore a propositional variable in which only this characteristic feature is constant.

4.127 The propositional variable signifies the formal concept, and its values signify the objects which fall under this concept.

4.1271 Every variable is the sign of a formal concept.

For every variable presents a constant form, which all its values possess, and which can be conceived as a formal property of these values.

4.1272   So the variable name "x" is the proper sign of the pseudo-concept *object*.

Wherever the word "object" ("thing", "entity", etc.) is rightly used, it is expressed in logical symbolism by the variable name. For example in the proposition "there are two objects which ...", by "$(\exists x, y) \ldots$".

Wherever it is used otherwise, *i.e.* as a proper concept word, there arise senseless pseudo-propositions.

So one cannot, *e.g.* say "There are objects" as one says "There are books". Nor "There are 100 objects" or "There are $\aleph_0$ objects". And it is senseless to speak of the *number of all objects*.

The same holds of the words "Complex", "Fact", "Function", "Number", etc.

They all signify formal concepts and are presented in logical symbolism by variables, not by functions or classes (as Frege and Russell thought).

Expressions like "1 is a number", "there is only one number nought", and all like them are senseless.

(It is as senseless to say, "there is only one 1" as it would be to say: $2 + 2$ is at 3 o'clock equal to 4.)

4.12721 The formal concept is already given with an object, which falls under it. One cannot, therefore, introduce both, the objects which fall under a formal concept *and* the formal concept itself, as primitive ideas. One cannot, therefore, *e.g.* introduce (as Russell does) the concept of function and also special functions as primitive ideas; or the concept of number and definite numbers.

4.1273   If we want to express in logical symbolism the general proposition "b is a successor of a" we need for this an expression for the general term of the formal series: aRb, $(\exists x) : aRx \cdot xRb$, $(\exists x, y) : aRx \cdot xRy \cdot yRb, \ldots$ The general term of a formal series can only be expressed by a variable, for the concept symbolized by "term of this formal series" is a *formal* concept. (This Frege and Russell overlooked; the way in which they express general propositions like the above is, therefore, false; it contains a vicious circle.)

We can determine the general term of the formal series by

48

giving its first term and the general form of the operation, which generates the following term out of the preceding proposition.

4.1274　The question about the existence of a formal concept is senseless. For no proposition can answer such a question.

(For example, one cannot ask: "Are there unanalysable subject-predicate propositions?")

4.128　The logical forms are *anumerical*.

Therefore there are in logic no pre-eminent numbers, and therefore there is no philosophical monism or dualism, etc.

4.2　The sense of a proposition is its agreement and disagreement with the possibilities of the existence and non-existence of the atomic facts.

4.21　The simplest proposition, the elementary proposition, asserts the existence of an atomic fact.

4.211　It is a sign of an elementary proposition, that no elementary proposition can contradict it.

4.22　The elementary proposition consists of names. It is a connexion, a concatenation, of names.

4.221　It is obvious that in the analysis of propositions we must come to elementary propositions, which consist of names in immediate combination.

The question arises here, how the propositional connexion comes to be.

4.2211　Even if the world is infinitely complex, so that every fact consists of an infinite number of atomic facts and every atomic fact is composed of an infinite number of objects, even then there must be objects and atomic facts.

4.23　The name occurs in the proposition only in the context of the elementary proposition.

4.24　The names are the simple symbols, I indicate them by single letters (x, y, z).

The elementary proposition I write as function of the names, in the form "fx", "$\phi(x, y)$", etc.

Or I indicate it by the letters p, q, r.

4.241   If I use two signs with one and the same meaning, I express this by putting between them the sign "=".

"$a = b$" means then, that the sign "a" is replaceable by the sign "b".

(If I introduce by an equation a new sign "b", by determining that it shall replace a previously known sign "a", I write the equation—definition—(like Russell) in the form "$a = b$ Def.". A definition is a symbolic rule.)

4.242   Expressions of the form "$a = b$" are therefore only expedients in presentation: They assert nothing about the meaning of the signs "a" and "b".

4.243   Can we understand two names without knowing whether they signify the same thing or two different things? Can we understand a proposition in which two names occur, without knowing if they mean the same or different things?

If I know the meaning of an English and a synonymous German word, it is impossible for me not to know that they are synonymous, it is impossible for me not to be able to translate them into one another.

Expressions like "$a = a$", or expressions deduced from these are neither elementary propositions nor otherwise significant signs. (This will be shown later.)

4.25   If the elementary proposition is true, the atomic fact exists; if it is false the atomic fact does not exist.

4.26   The specification of all true elementary propositions describes the world completely. The world is completely described by the specification of all elementary propositions plus the specification, which of them are true and which false.

4.27   With regard to the existence of n atomic facts there are $K_n = \sum_{\nu=0}^{n} \binom{n}{\nu}$ possibilities.

It is possible for all combinations of atomic facts to exist, and the others not to exist.

4.28   To these combinations correspond the same number of possibilities of the truth—and falsehood—of n elementary propositions.

4.3   The truth-possibilities of the elementary propositions mean the possibilities of the existence and non-existence of the atomic facts.

4.31 The truth-possibilities can be presented by schemata of the following kind ("T" means "true", "F" "false". The rows of T's and F's under the row of the elementary propositions mean their truth-possibilities in an easily intelligible symbolism).

p	q	r
T	T	T
F	T	T
T	F	T
T	T	F
F	F	T
F	T	F
T	F	F
F	F	F

p	q
T	T
F	T
T	F
F	F

p
T
F

4.4 A proposition is the expression of agreement and disagreement with the truth-possibilities of the elementary propositions.

4.41 The truth-possibilities of the elementary propositions are the conditions of the truth and falsehood of the propositions.

4.411 It seems probable even at first sight that the introduction of the elementary propositions is fundamental for the comprehension of the other kinds of propositions. Indeed the comprehension of the general propositions depends *palpably* on that of the elementary propositions.

4.42 With regard to the agreement and disagreement of a proposition with the truth-possibilities of n elementary propositions there are $\sum_{\kappa=0}^{K_n} \binom{K_n}{\kappa} = L_n$ possibilities.

4.43 Agreement with the truth-possibilities can be expressed by co-ordinating with them in the schema the mark "T" (true).

Absence of this mark means disagreement.

4.431 The expression of the agreement and disagreement with the truth-possibilities of the elementary propositions expresses the truth-conditions of the proposition.

The proposition is the expression of its truth-conditions.

(Frege has therefore quite rightly put them at the beginning, as explaining the signs of his logical symbolism. Only Frege's explanation of the truth-concept is false: if "the true" and "the false" were real objects and the arguments in $\sim p$, etc., then the sense of $\sim p$ would by no means be determined by Frege's determination.)

4.44   The sign which arises from the co-ordination of that mark "T" with the truth-possibilities is a propositional sign.

4.441   It is clear that to the complex of the signs "F" and "T" no object (or complex of objects) corresponds; any more than to horizontal and vertical lines or to brackets. There are no "logical objects"

Something analogous holds of course for all signs, which express the same as the schemata of "T" and "F".

4.442   Thus *e.g.*

"
p	q	
T	T	T
F	T	T
T	F	
F	F	T

"

    is a propositional sign.

(Frege's assertion sign "⊢" is logically altogether meaningless; in Frege (and Russell) it only shows that these authors hold as true the propositions marked in this way.

"⊢" belongs therefore to the propositions no more than does the number of the proposition. A proposition cannot possibly assert of itself that it is true.)

If the sequence of the truth-possibilities in the schema is once for all determined by a rule of combination, then the last column is by itself an expression of the truth-conditions. If we write this column as a row the propositional sign becomes: "(TT–T)(p, q)", or more plainly: "(TTFT)(p, q)".

(The number of places in the left-hand bracket is determined by the number of terms in the right-hand bracket.)

4.45   For n elementary propositions there are L_n possible groups of truth-conditions.

The groups of truth-conditions which belong to the truth-possibilities of a number of elementary propositions can be ordered in a series.

4.46 Among the possible groups of truth-conditions there are two extreme cases.

In the one case the proposition is true for all the truth-possibilities of the elementary propositions. We say that the truth-conditions are *tautological*.

In the second case the proposition is false for all the truth-possibilities. The truth-conditions are *self-contradictory*.

In the first case we call the proposition a tautology, in the second case a contradiction.

4.461 The proposition shows what it says, the tautology and the contradiction that they say nothing.

The tautology has no truth-conditions, for it is unconditionally true; and the contradiction is on no condition true.

Tautology and contradiction are without sense.

(Like the point from which two arrows go out in opposite directions.)

(I know, *e.g.* nothing about the weather, when I know that it rains or does not rain.)

4.4611 Tautology and contradiction are, however, not senseless; they are part of the symbolism, in the same way that "0" is part of the symbolism of Arithmetic.

4.462 Tautology and contradiction are not pictures of the reality. They present no possible state of affairs. For the one allows *every* possible state of affairs, the other *none*.

In the tautology the conditions of agreement with the world —the presenting relations—cancel one another, so that it stands in no presenting relation to reality.

4.463 The truth-conditions determine the range, which is left to the facts by the proposition.

(The proposition, the picture, the model, are in a negative sense like a solid body, which restricts the free movement of another: in a positive sense, like the space limited by solid substance, in which a body may be placed.)

Tautology leaves to reality the whole infinite logical space; contradiction fills the whole logical space and leaves no point to reality. Neither of them, therefore, can in any way determine reality.

4.464　The truth of tautology is certain, of propositions possible, of contradiction impossible. (Certain, possible, impossible: here we have an indication of that gradation which we need in the theory of probability.)

4.465　The logical product of a tautology and a proposition says the same as the proposition. Therefore that product is identical with the proposition. For the essence of the symbol cannot be altered without altering its sense.

4.466　To a definite logical combination of signs corresponds a definite logical combination of their meanings; *every arbitrary* combination only corresponds to the unconnected signs.

That is, propositions which are true for every state of affairs cannot be combinations of signs at all, for otherwise there could only correspond to them definite combinations of objects.

(And to no logical combination corresponds *no* combination of the objects.)

Tautology and contradiction are the limiting cases of the combinations of symbols, namely their dissolution.

4.4661　Of course the signs are also combined with one another in the tautology and contradiction, *i.e.* they stand in relations to one another, but these relations are meaningless, unessential to the *symbol.*

4.5　Now it appears to be possible to give the most general form of proposition; *i.e.* to give a description of the propositions of some one sign language, so that every possible sense can be expressed by a symbol, which falls under the description, and so that every symbol which falls under the description can express a sense, if the meanings of the names are chosen accordingly.

It is clear that in the description of the most general form of proposition *only* what is essential to it may be described—otherwise it would not be the most general form.

That there is a general form is proved by the fact that there cannot be a proposition whose form could not have been foreseen (*i.e.* constructed). The general form of proposition is: Such and such is the case.

4.51 Suppose *all* elementary propositions were given me: then we can simply ask: what propositions I can build out of them. And these are *all* propositions and *so* are they limited.

4.52 The propositions are everything which follows from the totality of all elementary propositions (of course also from the fact that it is the *totality of them all*). (So, in some sense, one could say, that *all* propositions are generalizations of the elementary propositions.)

4.53 The general propositional form is a variable.

5 Propositions are truth-functions of elementary propositions.

(An elementary proposition is a truth-function of itself.)

5.01 The elementary propositions are the truth-arguments of propositions.

5.02 It is natural to confuse the arguments of functions with the indices of names. For I recognize the meaning of the sign containing it from the argument just as much as from the index.

In Russell's "$+_c$", for example, "c" is an index which indicates that the whole sign is the addition sign for cardinal numbers. But this way of symbolizing depends on arbitrary agreement, and one could choose a simple sign instead of "$+_c$": but in "$\sim p$" "p" is not an index but an argument; the sense of "$\sim p$" *cannot* be understood, unless the sense of "p" has previously been understood. (In the name Julius Cæsar, Julius is an index. The index is always part of a description of the object to whose name we attach it, *e.g. The* Cæsar of the Julian gens.)

The confusion of argument and index is, if I am not mistaken, at the root of Frege's theory of the meaning of propositions and functions. For Frege the propositions of logic were names and their arguments the indices of these names.

5.1 The truth-functions can be ordered in series.

That is the foundation of the theory of probability.

5.101   The truth-functions of every number of elementary propositions can be written in a schema of the following kind:

(TTTT)(p, q) Tautology   (if p then p, and if q then q) $[p \supset p . q \supset q]$
(FTTT)(p, q) in words: Not both p and q. $[\sim(p . q)]$
(TFTT)(p, q) „   „   If q then p. $[q \supset p]$
(TTFT)(p, q) „   „   If p then q. $[p \supset q]$
(TTTF)(p, q) „   „ p or q. $[p \lor q]$
(FFTT)(p, q) „   „   Not q. $[\sim q]$
(FTFT)(p, q) „   „   Not p. $[\sim p]$
(FTTF)(p, q) „   „ p or q, but not both. $[p . \sim q : \lor : q . \sim p]$
(TFFT)(p, q) „   „   If p, then q; and if q, then p. $[p \equiv q]$
(TFTF)(p, q) „   „ p
(TTFF)(p, q) „   „ q
(FFFT)(p, q) „   „   Neither p nor q. $[\sim p . \sim q$ or $p \mid q]$
(FFTF)(p, q) „   „ p and not q. $[p . \sim q]$
(FTFF)(p, q) „   „ q and not p. $[q . \sim p]$
(TFFF)(p, q) „   „ p and q. $[p . q]$
(FFFF)(p, q) Contradiction (p and not p; and q and not q.) $[p . \sim p . q . \sim q]$

Those truth-possibilities of its truth-arguments, which verify the proposition, I shall call its *truth-grounds*.

5.11   If the truth-grounds which are common to a number of propositions are all also truth-grounds of some one proposition, we say that the truth of this proposition follows from the truth of those propositions.

5.12   In particular the truth of a proposition p follows from that of a proposition q, if all the truth-grounds of the second are truth-grounds of the first.

5.121   The truth-grounds of q are contained in those of p; p follows from q.

5.122   If p follows from q, the sense of "p" is contained in that of "q".

5.123   If a god creates a world in which certain propositions are true, he creates thereby also a world in which all propositions consequent on them are true. And similarly he could not create a world in which the proposition "p" is true without creating all its objects.

5.124   A proposition asserts every proposition which follows from it.

5.1241   "$p . q$" is one of the propositions which assert "p" and at the same time one of the propositions which assert "q".

Two propositions are opposed to one another if there is no significant proposition which asserts them both.

Every proposition which contradicts another, denies it.

5.13   That the truth of one proposition follows from the truth of other propositions, we perceive from the structure of the propositions.

5.131   If the truth of one proposition follows from the truth of others, this expresses itself in relations in which the forms of these propositions stand to one another, and we do not need to put them in these relations first by connecting them with one another in a proposition; for these relations are internal, and exist as soon as, and by the very fact that, the propositions exist.

5.1311   When we conclude from $p \vee q$ and $\sim p$ to q the relation between the forms of the propositions "$p \vee q$" and "$\sim p$" is here concealed by the method of symbolizing. But if we write, $e.g.$ instead of "$p \vee q$" "$p \mid q . \mid . p \mid q$" and instead of "$\sim p$" "$p \mid p$" ($p \mid q$ = neither p nor q), then the inner connexion becomes obvious.

(The fact that we can infer fa from $(x) . fx$ shows that generality is present also in the symbol "$(x) . fx$".

5.132   If p follows from q, I can conclude from q to p; infer p from q.

The method of inference is to be understood from the two propositions alone.

Only they themselves can justify the inference.

Laws of inference, which—as in Frege and Russell—are to justify the conclusions, are senseless and would be superfluous.

5.133   All inference takes place a priori.

5.134   From an elementary proposition no other can be inferred.

5.135   In no way can an inference be made from the existence of one state of affairs to the existence of another entirely different from it.

5.136   There is no causal nexus which justifies such an inference.

5.1361   The events of the future $cannot$ be inferred from those of the present.

Superstition is the belief in the causal nexus.

5.1362   The freedom of the will consists in the fact that future actions cannot be known now. We could only know them if causality were an *inner* necessity, like that of logical deduction.—The connexion of knowledge and what is known is that of logical necessity.

("A knows that *p* is the case" is senseless if *p* is a tautology.)

5.1363 If from the fact that a proposition is obvious to us it does not *follow* that it is true, then obviousness is no justification for our belief in its truth.

5.14 If a proposition follows from another, then the latter says more than the former, the former less than the latter.

5.141 If *p* follows from *q* and *q* from *p* then they are one and the same proposition.

5.142 A tautology follows from all propositions: it says nothing.

5.143 Contradiction is something shared by propositions, which *no* proposition has in common with another. Tautology is that which is shared by all propositions, which have nothing in common with one another.

Contradiction vanishes so to speak outside, tautology inside all propositions.

Contradiction is the external limit of the propositions, tautology their substanceless centre.

5.15 If T_r is the number of the truth-grounds of the proposition "*r*", T_{rs} the number of those truth-grounds of the proposition "*s*" which are at the same time truth-grounds of "*r*", then we call the ratio $T_{rs} : T_r$ the measure of the probability which the proposition "*r*" gives to the proposition "*s*".

5.151 Suppose in a schema like that above in No. 5.101 T_r is the number of the "T"'s in the proposition *r*, T_{rs} the number of those "T"'s in the proposition *s*, which stand in the same columns as "T"'s of the proposition *r*; then the proposition *r* gives to the proposition *s* the probability $T_{rs} : T_r$.

5.1511 There is no special object peculiar to probability propositions.

5.152 Propositions which have no truth-arguments in common with one another we call independent.

Independent propositions (*e.g.* any two elementary propositions) give to one another the probability $\frac{1}{2}$.

If *p* follows from *q*, the proposition *q* gives to the proposition *p* the probability 1. The certainty of logical conclusion is a limiting case of probability.

(Application to tautology and contradiction.)

5.153 A proposition is in itself neither probable nor improbable. An event occurs or does not occur, there is no middle course.

5.154 In an urn there are equal numbers of white and black balls (and no others). I draw one ball after another and put them back in the urn. Then I can determine by the experiment that the numbers of the black and white balls which are drawn approximate as the drawing continues.

So *this* is not a mathematical fact.

If then, I say, It is equally probable that I should draw a white and a black ball, this means, All the circumstances known to me (including the natural laws hypothetically assumed) give to the occurrence of the one event no more probability than to the occurrence of the other. That is they give—as can easily be understood from the above explanations—to each the probability $\frac{1}{2}$.

What I can verify by the experiment is that the occurrence of the two events is independent of the circumstances with which I have no closer acquaintance.

5.155 The unit of the probability proposition is: The circumstances—with which I am not further acquainted—give to the occurrence of a definite event such and such a degree of probability.

5.156 Probability is a generalization.

It involves a general description of a propositional form. Only in default of certainty do we need probability.

If we are not completely acquainted with a fact, but know *something* about its form.

(A proposition can, indeed, be an incomplete picture of a certain state of affairs, but it is always *a* complete picture.)

The probability proposition is, as it were, an extract from other propositions.

5.2 The structures of propositions stand to one another in internal relations.

5.21 We can bring out these internal relations in our manner of expression, by presenting a proposition as the result of an operation which produces it from other propositions (the bases of the operation).

5.22 The operation is the expression of a relation between the structures of its result and its bases.

5.23 The operation is that which must happen to a proposition in order to make another out of it.

5.231 And that will naturally depend on their formal properties, on the internal similarity of their forms.

5.232 The internal relation which orders a series is equivalent to the operation by which one term arises from another.

5.233 The first place in which an operation can occur is where a proposition arises from another in a logically significant way; *i.e.* where the logical construction of the proposition begins.

5.234 The truth-functions of elementary propositions, are results of operations which have the elementary propositions as bases. (I call these operations, truth-operations.)

5.2341 The sense of a truth-function of p is a function of the sense of p.
    Denial, logical addition, logical multiplication, etc. etc., are operations.
    (Denial reverses the sense of a proposition.)

5.24 An operation shows itself in a variable; it shows how we can proceed from one form of proposition to another.
    It gives expression to the difference between the forms.
    (And that which is common to the bases, and the result of an operation, is the bases themselves.)

5.241 The operation does not characterize a form but only the difference between forms.

5.242 The same operation which makes "q" from "p", makes "r" from "q", and so on. This can only be expressed by the fact that "p", "q", "r", etc., are variables which give general expression to certain formal relations.

5.25 The occurrence of an operation does not characterize the sense of a proposition.

For an operation does not assert anything; only its result does, and this depends on the bases of the operation.

(Operation and function must not be confused with one another.)

5.251 A function cannot be its own argument, but the result of an operation can be its own basis.

5.252 Only in this way is the progress from term to term in a formal series possible (from type to type in the hierarchy of Russell and Whitehead). (Russell and Whitehead have not admitted the possibility of this progress but have made use of it all the same.)

5.2521 The repeated application of an operation to its own result I call its successive application ("$O'O'O'a$" is the result of the threefold successive application of "$O'\xi$" to "a").

In a similar sense I speak of the successive application of *several* operations to a number of propositions.

5.2522 The general term of the formal series $a, O'a, O'O'a, \ldots$ I write thus: "$|a, x, O'x|$". This expression in brackets is a variable. The first term of the expression is the beginning of the formal series, the second the form of an arbitrary term x of the series, and the third the form of that term of the series which immediately follows x.

5.2523 The concept of the successive application of an operation is equivalent to the concept "and so on".

5.253 One operation can reverse the effect of another. Operations can cancel one another.

5.254 Operations can vanish (*e.g.* denial in "$\sim\sim p$", $\sim\sim p = p$).

5.3 All propositions are results of truth-operations on the elementary propositions.

The truth-operation is the way in which a truth-function arises from elementary propositions.

According to the nature of truth-operations, in the same way as out of elementary propositions arise their truth-functions, from truth-functions arises a new one. Every truth-operation creates from truth-functions of elementary propositions another truth-function of elementary propositions, *i.e.* a proposition. The result of every truth-operation on the results of truth-operations on elementary propositions is also the result of *one* truth-operation on elementary propositions.

Every proposition is the result of truth-operations on elementary propositions.

5.31   The Schemata No. 4.31 are also significant, if "*p*", "*q*", "*r*", etc. are not elementary propositions.

And it is easy to see that the propositional sign in No. 4.442 expresses one truth-function of elementary propositions even when "*p*" and "*q*" are truth-functions of elementary propositions.

5.32   All truth-functions are results of the successive application of a finite number of truth-operations to elementary propositions.

5.4   Here it becomes clear that there are no such things as "logical objects" or "logical constants" (in the sense of Frege and Russell).

5.41   For all those results of truth-operations on truth-functions are identical, which are one and the same truth-function of elementary propositions.

5.42   That ∨, ⊃, etc., are not relations in the sense of right and left, etc., is obvious.

The possibility of crosswise definition of the logical "primitive signs" of Frege and Russell shows by itself that these are not primitive signs and that they signify no relations.

And it is obvious that the "⊃" which we define by means of "∼" and "∨" is identical with that by which we define "∨" with the help of "∼", and that this "∨" is the same as the first, and so on.

5.43   That from a fact *p* an infinite number of *others* should follow, namely ∼∼*p*, ∼∼∼∼*p*, etc., is indeed hardly to be believed, and it is no less wonderful that the infinite number of propositions of logic (of mathematics) should follow from half a dozen "primitive propositions".

But all propositions of logic say the same thing. That is, nothing.

5.44   Truth-functions are not material functions.

If *e.g.* an affirmation can be produced by repeated denial, is the denial—in any sense—contained in the affirmation?

Does "$\sim\sim p$" deny $\sim p$, or does it affirm p; or both?

The proposition "$\sim\sim p$" does not treat of denial as an object, but the possibility of denial is already prejudged in affirmation.

And if there was an object called "$\sim$", then "$\sim\sim p$" would have to say something other than "p". For the one proposition would then treat of $\sim$, the other would not.

5.441   This disappearance of the apparent logical constants also occurs if "$\sim(\exists x).\sim fx$" says the same as "$(x).fx$", or "$(\exists x).fx.x = a$" the same as "fa".

5.442   If a proposition is given to us then the results of all truth-operations which have it as their basis are given *with* it.

5.45   If there are logical primitive signs a correct logic must make clear their position relative to one another and justify their existence. The construction of logic *out of* its primitive signs must become clear.

5.451   If logic has primitive ideas these must be independent of one another. If a primitive idea is introduced it must be introduced in all contexts in which it occurs at all. One cannot therefore introduce it for *one* context and then again for another. For example, if denial is introduced, we must understand it in propositions of the form "$\sim p$", just as in propositions like "$\sim(p\vee q)$", "$(\exists x).\sim fx$" and others. We may not first introduce it for one class of cases and then for another, for it would then remain doubtful whether its meaning in the two cases was the same, and there would be no reason to use the same way of symbolizing in the two cases.

(In short, what Frege ("Grundgesetze der Arithmetik") has said about the introduction of signs by definitions holds, mutatis mutandis, for the introduction of primitive signs also.)

5.452   The introduction of a new expedient in the symbolism of logic must always be an event full of consequences. No new symbol may be introduced in logic in brackets or in the margin—with, so to speak, an entirely innocent face.

(Thus in the "Principia Mathematica" of Russell and Whitehead there occur definitions and primitive propositions in words. Why suddenly words here? This would need a justification. There was none, and can be none for the process is actually not allowed.)

But if the introduction of a new expedient has proved necessary in one place, we must immediately ask: Where is this expedient *always* to be used? Its position in logic must be made clear.

5.453 All numbers in logic must be capable of justification.

Or rather it must become plain that there are no numbers in logic.

There are no pre-eminent numbers.

5.454 In logic there is no side by side, there can be no classification.

In logic there cannot be a more general and a more special.

5.4541 The solution of logical problems must be simple for they set the standard of simplicity.

Men have always thought that there must be a sphere of questions whose answers—a priori—are symmetrical and united into a closed regular structure.

A sphere in which the proposition, simplex sigillum veri, is valid.

5.46 When we have rightly introduced the logical signs, the sense of all their combinations has been already introduced with them: therefore not only "$p \vee q$" but also "$\sim(p \vee \sim q)$", etc. etc. We should then already have introduced the effect of all possible combinations of brackets; and it would then have become clear that the proper general primitive signs are not "$p \vee q$", "$(\exists x) . fx$", etc., but the most general form of their combinations.

5.461 The apparently unimportant fact that the apparent relations like $\vee$ and $\supset$ need brackets—unlike real relations is of great importance.

The use of brackets with these apparent primitive signs shows that these are not the real primitive signs; and nobody of course would believe that the brackets have meaning by themselves.

5.4611 Logical operation signs are punctuations.

5.47 It is clear that everything which can be said *beforehand* about the form of *all* propositions at all can be said *on one occasion.*

For all logical operations are already contained in the elementary proposition. For "fa" says the same as "$(\exists x) . fx . x = a$".

Where there is composition, there is argument and function, and where these are, all logical constants already are.

One could say: the one logical constant is that which *all* propositions, according to their nature, have in common with one another.

That however is the general form of proposition.

5.471 The general form of proposition is the essence of proposition.

5.4711 To give the essence of proposition means to give the essence of all description, therefore the essence of the world.

5.472 The description of the most general propositional form is the description of the one and only general primitive sign in logic.

5.473 Logic must take care of itself.

A *possible* sign must also be able to signify. Everything which is possible in logic is also permitted. ("Socrates is identical" means nothing because there is no property which is called "identical". The proposition is senseless because we have not made some arbitrary determination, not because the symbol is in itself unpermissible.)

In a certain sense we cannot make mistakes in logic.

5.4731 Self-evidence, of which Russell has said so much, can only be discarded in logic by language itself preventing every logical mistake. That logic is a priori consists in the fact that we *cannot* think illogically.

5.4732 We cannot give a sign the wrong sense.

5.47321 Occam's razor is, of course, not an arbitrary rule nor one justified by its practical success. It simply says that *unnecessary* elements in a symbolism mean nothing.

Signs which serve *one* purpose are logically equivalent, signs which serve *no* purpose are logically meaningless.

5.4733 Frege says: Every legitimately constructed proposition must have a sense; and I say: Every possible proposition is legitimately constructed, and if it has no sense this can only be because we have given no *meaning* to some of its constituent parts.

(Even if we believe that we have done so.)

Thus "Socrates is identical" says nothing, because we have given *no* meaning to the word "identical" as *adjective*. For when it occurs as the sign of equality it symbolizes in an entirely different way—the symbolizing relation is another—therefore the symbol is in the two cases entirely different; the two symbols have the sign in common with one another only by accident.

5.474   The number of necessary fundamental operations depends *only* on our notation.

5.475   It is only a question of constructing a system of signs of a definite number of dimensions—of a definite mathematical multiplicity.

5.476   It is clear that we are not concerned here with a *number of primitive ideas* which must be signified but with the expression of a rule.

5.5   Every truth-function is a result of the successive application of the operation $(- - - - -T)(\xi, \ldots)$ to elementary propositions.

This operation denies all the propositions in the right-hand bracket and I call it the negation of these propositions.

5.501   An expression in brackets whose terms are propositions I indicate—if the order of the terms in the bracket is indifferent—by a sign of the form "$(\bar{\xi})$". "ξ" is a variable whose values are the terms of the expression in brackets, and the line over the variable indicates that it stands for all its values in the bracket.

(Thus if ξ has the 3 values P, Q, R, then $(\bar{\xi}) = (P, Q, R)$.)

The values of the variables must be determined.

The determination is the description of the propositions which the variable stands for.

How the description of the terms of the expression in brackets takes place is unessential.

We may distinguish 3 kinds of description: 1. Direct enumeration. In this case we can place simply its constant values instead of the variable. 2. Giving a function fx, whose values for all values of x are the propositions to be described. 3. Giving a formal law, according to which those propositions are constructed. In this case the terms of the expression in brackets are all the terms of a formal series.

5.502   Therefore I write instead of "$(- - - - -T)(\xi, \ldots)$", "$N(\overline{\xi})$".

$N(\overline{\xi})$ is the negation of all the values of the propositional variable ξ.

5.503   As it is obviously easy to express how propositions can be constructed by means of this operation and how propositions are not to be constructed by means of it, this must be capable of exact expression.

5.51   If ξ has only one value, then $N(\overline{\xi}) = \sim p$ (not p), if it has two values then $N(\overline{\xi}) = \sim p \,.\, \sim q$ (neither p nor q).

5.511   How can the all-embracing logic which mirrors the world use such special catches and manipulations? Only because all these are connected into an infinitely fine network, to the great mirror.

5.512   "$\sim p$" is true if "p" is false. Therefore in the true proposition "$\sim p$" "p" is a false proposition. How then can the stroke "$\sim$" bring it into agreement with reality?

That which denies in "$\sim p$" is however not "$\sim$", but that which all signs of this notation, which deny p, have in common.

Hence the common rule according to which "$\sim p$", "$\sim\sim\sim p$", "$\sim p \vee \sim p$", "$\sim p \,.\, \sim p$", etc. etc. (to infinity) are constructed. And this which is common to them all mirrors denial.

5.513   We could say: What is common to all symbols, which assert both p and q, is the proposition "$p \,.\, q$". What is common to all symbols, which assert either p or q, is the proposition "$p \vee q$".

And similarly we can say: Two propositions are opposed to one another when they have nothing in common with one another; and every proposition has only one negative, because there is only one proposition which lies altogether outside it.

Thus even in Russell's notation it is evident that "$q : p \vee \sim p$" says the same as "q"; that "$p \vee \sim p$" says nothing.

5.514   If a notation is fixed, there is in it a rule according to which all the propositions denying p are constructed, a rule according to which all the propositions asserting p are constructed, a rule according to which all the propositions asserting p or q are constructed, and so on. These rules are equivalent to the symbols and in them their sense is mirrored.

5.515　It must be recognized in our symbols that what is connected by "$\lor$", ".", etc., must be propositions.

And this is the case, for the symbols "p" and "q" presuppose "$\lor$", "$\sim$", etc. If the sign "p" in "$p \lor q$" does not stand for a complex sign, then by itself it cannot have sense; but then also the signs "$p \lor p$", "$p . p$", etc. which have the same sense as "p" have no sense. If, however, "$p \lor p$" has no sense, then also "$p \lor q$" can have no sense.

5.5151　Must the sign of the negative proposition be constructed by means of the sign of the positive? Why should one not be able to express the negative proposition by means of a negative fact? (Like: if "a" does not stand in a certain relation to "b", it could express that aRb is not the case.)

But here also the negative proposition is indirectly constructed with the positive.

The positive *proposition* must presuppose the existence of the negative *proposition* and conversely.

5.52　If the values of ξ are the total values of a function fx for all values of x, then $N(\overline{\xi}) = \sim(\exists x) . fx$.

5.521　I separate the concept *all* from the truth-function.

Frege and Russell have introduced generality in connexion with the logical product or the logical sum. Then it would be difficult to understand the propositions "$(\exists x) . fx$" and "$(x) . fx$" in which both ideas lie concealed.

5.522　That which is peculiar to the "symbolism of generality" is firstly, that it refers to a logical prototype, and secondly, that it makes constants prominent.

5.523　The generality symbol occurs as an argument.

5.524　If the objects are given, therewith are *all* objects also given.

If the elementary propositions are given, then therewith *all* elementary propositions are also given.

5.525　It is not correct to render the proposition "$(\exists x) . fx$"—as Russell does—in words "fx is *possible*".

Certainty, possibility or impossibility of a state of affairs are not expressed by a proposition but by the fact that an expression is a tautology, a significant proposition or a contradiction.

That precedent to which one would always appeal, must be present in the symbol itself.

5.526 One can describe the world completely by completely generalized propositions, *i.e.* without from the outset co-ordinating any name with a definite object.

In order then to arrive at the customary way of expression we need simply say after an expression "there is one and only one x, which ....": and this x is a.

5.5261 A completely generalized proposition is like every other proposition composite. (This is shown by the fact that in "$(\exists x, \phi) . \phi x$" we must mention "$\phi$" and "$x$" separately. Both stand independently in signifying relations to the world as in the ungeneralized proposition.)

A characteristic of a composite symbol: it has something in common with *other* symbols.

5.5262 The truth or falsehood of *every* proposition alters something in the general structure of the world. And the range which is allowed to its structure by the totality of elementary propositions is exactly that which the completely general propositions delimit.

(If an elementary proposition is true, then, at any rate, there is one *more* elementary proposition true.)

5.53 Identity of the object I express by identity of the sign and not by means of a sign of identity. Difference of the objects by difference of the signs.

5.5301 That identity is not a relation between objects is obvious. This becomes very clear if, for example, one considers the proposition "$(x) : fx . \supset .x = a$". What this proposition says is simply that *only* a satisfies the function f, and not that only such things satisfy the function f which have a certain relation to a.

One could of course say that in fact *only* a has this relation to a, but in order to express this we should need the sign of identity itself.

69

5.5302 Russell's definition of "$=$" won't do; because according to it one cannot say that two objects have all their properties in common. (Even if this proposition is never true, it is nevertheless *significant.*)

5.5303 Roughly speaking: to say of *two* things that they are identical is nonsense, and to say of *one* thing that it is identical with itself is to say nothing.

5.531 I write therefore not "$f(a,b) \cdot a = b$", but "$f(a,a)$" (or "$f(b,b)$"). And not "$f(a,b) \cdot \sim a = b$", but "$f(a,b)$".

5.532 And analogously: not "$(\exists x, y).f(x,y).x = y$", but "$(\exists x).f(x,x)$"; and not "$(\exists x, y) \cdot f(x,y) \cdot \sim x = y$", but "$(\exists x, y) \cdot f(x,y)$".

(Therefore instead of Russell's "$(\exists x, y) \cdot f(x,y)$": "$(\exists x, y) \cdot f(x,y) \cdot \vee \cdot (\exists x) \cdot f(x,x)$".)

5.5321 Instead of "$(x) : fx \supset x = a$" we therefore write e.g. "$(\exists x).fx \cdot \supset \cdot fa : \sim(\exists x, y) \cdot fx \cdot fy$".

And the proposition "*only* one x satisfies $f()$" reads: "$(\exists x) \cdot fx : \sim(\exists x, y) \cdot fx \cdot fy$".

5.533 The identity sign is therefore not an essential constituent of logical notation.

5.534 And we see that apparent propositions like: "$a = a$", "$a = b \cdot b = c \cdot \supset a = c$", "$(x) \cdot x = x$", "$(\exists x) \cdot x = a$", etc. cannot be written in a correct logical notation at all.

5.535 So all problems disappear which are connected with such pseudo-propositions.

This is the place to solve all the problems which arise through Russell's "Axiom of Infinity".

What the axiom of infinity is meant to say would be expressed in language by the fact that there is an infinite number of names with different meanings.

5.5351 There are certain cases in which one is tempted to use expressions of the form "$a = a$" or "$p \supset p$" and of that kind. And indeed this takes place when one would like to speak of the archetype Proposition, Thing, etc. So Russell in the *Principles of Mathematics* has rendered the nonsense "p is a proposition" in symbols by "$p \supset p$" and has put it as hypothesis before certain propositions to show that their places for arguments could only be occupied by propositions.

(It is nonsense to place the hypothesis $p \supset p$ before a proposition in order to ensure that its arguments have the right form, because the hypothesis for a non-proposition as argument becomes not false but meaningless, and because the proposition itself becomes senseless for arguments of the wrong kind, and therefore it survives the wrong arguments no better and no worse than the senseless hypothesis attached for this purpose.)

5.5352   Similarly it was proposed to express "There are no things" by "$\sim(\exists x) . x = x$". But even if this were a proposition—would it not be true if indeed "There were things", but these were not identical with themselves?

5.54   In the general propositional form, propositions occur in a proposition only as bases of the truth-operations.

5.541   At first sight it appears as if there were also a different way in which one proposition could occur in another.

Especially in certain propositional forms of psychology, like "A thinks, that p is the case", or "A thinks p", etc.

Here it appears superficially as if the proposition p stood to the object A in a kind of relation.

(And in modern epistemology (Russell, Moore, etc.) those propositions have been conceived in this way.)

5.542   But it is clear that "A believes that p", "A thinks p", "A says p", are of the form "'p' says p": and here we have no co-ordination of a fact and an object, but a co-ordination of facts by means of a co-ordination of their objects.

5.5421   This shows that there is no such thing as the soul—the subject, etc.—as it is conceived in contemporary superficial psychology.

A composite soul would not be a soul any longer.

5.5422   The correct explanation of the form of the proposition "A judges p" must show that it is impossible to judge a nonsense. (Russell's theory does not satisfy this condition.)

5.5423   To perceive a complex means to perceive that its constituents are combined in such and such a way.

This perhaps explains that the figure

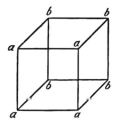

can be seen in two ways as a cube; and all similar phenomena. For we really see two different facts.

(If I fix my eyes first on the corners a and only glance at b, a appears in front and b behind, and vice versa.)

5.55　We must now answer a priori the question as to all possible forms of the elementary propositions.

The elementary proposition consists of names. Since we cannot give the number of names with different meanings, we cannot give the composition of the elementary proposition.

5.551　Our fundamental principle is that every question which can be decided at all by logic can be decided without further trouble.

(And if we get into a situation where we need to answer such a problem by looking at the world, this shows that we are on a fundamentally wrong track.)

5.552　The "experience" which we need to understand logic is not that such and such is the case, but that something *is*; but that is *no* experience.

Logic *precedes* every experience—that something is *so*.

It is before the How, not before the What.

5.5521　And if this were not the case, how could we apply logic? We could say: if there were a logic, even if there were no world, how then could there be a logic, since there is a world?

5.553　Russell said that there were simple relations between different numbers of things (individuals). But between what numbers? And how should this be decided—by experience?

(There is no pre-eminent number.)

5.554 The enumeration of any special forms would be entirely arbitrary.

5.5541 It should be possible to decide a priori whether, for example, I can get into a situation in which I need to symbolize with a sign of a 27-termed relation.

5.5542 May we then ask this at all? Can we set out a sign form and not know whether anything can correspond to it?

Has the question sense: what must *be* in order that something can be the case?

5.555 It is clear that we have a concept of the elementary proposition apart from its special logical form.

Where, however, we can build symbols according to a system, there this system is the logically important thing and not the single symbols.

And how would it be possible that I should have to deal with forms in logic which I can invent: but I must have to deal with that which makes it possible for me to invent them.

5.556 There cannot be a hierarchy of the forms of the elementary propositions. Only that which we ourselves construct can we foresee.

5.5561 Empirical reality is limited by the totality of objects. The boundary appears again in the totality of elementary propositions.

The hierarchies are and must be independent of reality.

5.5562 If we know on purely logical grounds, that there must be elementary propositions, then this must be known by everyone who understands the propositions in their unanalysed form.

5.5563 All propositions of our colloquial language are actually, just as they are, logically completely in order. That most simple thing which we ought to give here is not a simile of truth but the complete truth itself.

(Our problems are not abstract but perhaps the most concrete that there are.)

5.557 The *application* of logic decides what elementary propositions there are.

What lies in the application logic cannot anticipate.

It is clear that logic may not collide with its application.

But logic must have contact with its application.

Therefore logic and its application may not overlap one another.

5.5571 If I cannot give elementary propositions a priori then it must lead to obvious nonsense to try to give them.

5.6 *The limits of my language* mean the limits of my world.

5.61 Logic fills the world: the limits of the world are also its limits.

We cannot therefore say in logic: This and this there is in the world, that there is not.

For that would apparently presuppose that we exclude certain possibilities, and this cannot be the case since otherwise logic must get outside the limits of the world: that is, if it could consider these limits from the other side also.

What we cannot think, that we cannot think: we cannot therefore *say* what we cannot think.

5.62 This remark provides a key to the question, to what extent solipsism is a truth.

In fact what solipsism *means*, is quite correct, only it cannot be *said*, but it shows itself.

That the world is *my* world, shows itself in the fact that the limits of the language (the language which only I understand) mean the limits of *my* world.

5.621 The world and life are one.

5.63 I am my world. (The microcosm.)

5.631 The thinking, presenting subject; there is no such thing.

If I wrote a book "The world as I found it", I should also have therein to report on my body and say which members obey my will and which do not, etc. This then would be a method of isolating the subject or rather of showing that in an important sense there is no subject: that is to say, of it alone in this book mention could *not* be made.

5.632 The subject does not belong to the world but it is a limit of the world.

5.633 *Where in* the world is a metaphysical subject to be noted? You say that this case is altogether like that of the eye and the field of sight. But you do *not* really see the eye. And from nothing *in the field of sight* can it be concluded that it is seen from an eye.

5.6331 For the field of sight has not a form like this:

5.634 This is connected with the fact that no part of our experience is also a priori.

Everything we see could also be otherwise.

Everything we can describe at all could also be otherwise.

There is no order of things a priori.

5.64 Here we see that solipsism strictly carried out coincides with pure realism. The I in solipsism shrinks to an extensionless point and there remains the reality co-ordinated with it.

5.641 There is therefore really a sense in which in philosophy we can talk of a non-psychological I.

The I occurs in philosophy through the fact that the "world is my world".

The philosophical I is not the man, not the human body or the human soul of which psychology treats, but the metaphysical subject, the limit—not a part of the world.

6 The general form of truth-function is: $[\bar{p}, \bar{\xi}, N(\bar{\xi})]$.

This is the general form of proposition.

6.001 This says nothing else than that every proposition is the result of successive applications of the operation $N'(\bar{\xi})$ to the elementary propositions.

6.002 If we are given the general form of the way in which a proposition is constructed, then thereby we are also given the general form of the way in which by an operation out of one proposition another can be created.

6.01 The general form of the operation $\Omega'(\overline{\eta})$ is therefore: $[\overline{\xi}, N(\overline{\xi})]'(\overline{\eta})$ $(= [\overline{\eta}, \overline{\xi}, N(\overline{\xi})])$.

This is the most general form of transition from one proposition to another.

6.02 And thus we come to numbers: I define

$$x = \Omega^{0\prime}x \text{ Def. and}$$
$$\Omega'\Omega^{\nu\prime}x = \Omega^{\nu+1\prime}x \text{ Def.}$$

According, then, to these symbolic rules we write the series $x, \Omega'x, \Omega'\Omega'x, \Omega'\Omega'\Omega'x \ldots$

$$\text{as: } \Omega^{0\prime}x, \Omega^{0+1\prime}x, \Omega^{0+1+1\prime}x, \Omega^{0+1+1+1\prime}x \ldots$$

Therefore I write in place of "$[x, \xi, \Omega'\xi]$",

$$\text{"}[\Omega^{0\prime}x, \Omega^{\nu\prime}x, \Omega^{\nu+1\prime}x]\text{".}$$

And I define:

$$0 + 1 = 1 \text{ Def.}$$
$$0 + 1 + 1 = 2 \text{ Def.}$$
$$0 + 1 + 1 + 1 = 3 \text{ Def.}$$
and so on.

6.021 A number is the exponent of an operation.

6.022 The concept number is nothing else than that which is common to all numbers, the general form of number.

The concept number is the variable number.

And the concept of equality of numbers is the general form of all special equalities of numbers.

6.03 The general form of the cardinal number is: $[0, \xi, \xi + 1]$.

6.031 The theory of classes is altogether superfluous in mathematics.

This is connected with the fact that the generality which we need in mathematics is not the *accidental* one.

6.1 The propositions of logic are tautologies.

6.11 The propositions of logic therefore say nothing. (They are the analytical propositions.)

6.111 Theories which make a proposition of logic appear substantial are always false. One could *e.g.* believe that the words "true" and "false" signify two properties among other properties, and then it would appear as a remarkable fact that every proposition possesses one of these properties. This now by no means appears self-evident, no more so than the proposition "All roses are either yellow or red" would sound even if it were true. Indeed our proposition now gets quite the character of a proposition of natural science and this is a certain symptom of its being falsely understood.

6.112 The correct explanation of logical propositions must give them a peculiar position among all propositions.

6.113 It is the characteristic mark of logical propositions that one can perceive in the symbol alone that they are true; and this fact contains in itself the whole philosophy of logic. And so also it is one of the most important facts that the truth or falsehood of non-logical propositions can *not* be recognized from the propositions alone.

6.12 The fact that the propositions of logic are tautologies *shows* the formal—logical—properties of language, of the world.

That its constituent parts connected together *in this way* give a tautology characterizes the logic of its constituent parts.

In order that propositions connected together in a definite way may give a tautology they must have definite properties of structure. That they give a tautology when *so* connected shows therefore that they possess these properties of structure.

6.1201 That *e.g.* the propositions "p" and "$\sim p$" in the connexion "$\sim(p . \sim p)$" give a tautology shows that they contradict one another. That the propositions "$p \supset q$", "p" and "q" connected together in the form "$(p \supset q) . (p) :\supset: (q)$" give a tautology shows that q follows from p and $p \supset q$. That "$(x) . fx :\supset: fa$" is a tautology shows that fa follows from $(x) . fx$, etc. etc.

6.1202 It is clear that we could have used for this purpose contradictions instead of tautologies.

6.1203 In order to recognize a tautology as such, we can, in cases in which no sign of generality occurs in the tautology, make use of the following intuitive method: I write instead of "*p*", "*q*", "*r*", etc., "*TpF*", "*TqF*", "*TrF*", etc. The truth-combinations I express by brackets, *e.g.*:

and the co-ordination of the truth or falsity of the whole proposition with the truth-combinations of the truth-arguments by lines in the following way:

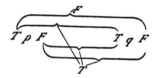

This sign, for example, would therefore present the proposition $p \supset q$. Now I will proceed to inquire whether such a proposition as $\sim(p \cdot \sim p)$ (The Law of Contradiction) is a tautology. The form "$\sim\xi$" is written in our notation

$$\text{``T}\xi\text{F''} \qquad \begin{matrix} \text{T} \\ \searrow \\ \text{F} \end{matrix}$$

the form "$\xi \cdot \eta$" thus:—

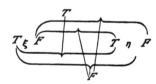

78

Hence the proposition $\sim(p \,.\, \sim q)$ runs thus:—

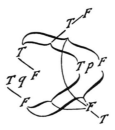

If here we put "p" instead of "q" and examine the combination of the outermost T and F with the innermost, it is seen that the truth of the whole proposition is co-ordinated with *all* the truth-combinations of its argument, its falsity with none of the truth-combinations.

6.121　The propositions of logic demonstrate the logical properties of propositions, by combining them into propositions which say nothing.

This method could be called a zero-method. In a logical proposition propositions are brought into equilibrium with one another, and the state of equilibrium then shows how these propositions must be logically constructed.

6.122　Whence it follows that we can get on without logical propositions, for we can recognize in an adequate notation the formal properties of the propositions by mere inspection.

6.1221　If for example two propositions "p" and "q" give a tautology in the connexion "$p \supset q$", then it is clear that q follows from p.

E.g. that "q" follows from "$p \supset q \,.\, p$" we see from these two propositions themselves, but we can also show it by combining them to "$p \supset q.p :\supset: q$" and then showing that this is a tautology.

6.1222　This throws light on the question why logical propositions can no more be empirically established than they can be empirically refuted. Not only must a proposition of logic be incapable of being contradicted by any possible experience, but it must also be incapable of being established by any such.

6.1223　It now becomes clear why we often feel as though "logical truths" must be "*postulated*" by us. We can in fact postulate them in so far as we can postulate an adequate notation.

6.1224　It also becomes clear why logic has been called the theory of forms and of inference.

6.123　It is clear that the laws of logic cannot themselves obey further logical laws.

　　　　(There is not, as Russell supposed, for every "type" a special law of contradiction; but one is sufficient, since it is not applied to itself.)

6.1231　The mark of logical propositions is not their general validity.

　　　　To be general is only to be accidentally valid for all things. An ungeneralized proposition can be tautologous just as well as a generalized one.

6.1232　Logical general validity, we could call essential as opposed to accidental general validity, *e.g.* of the proposition "all men are mortal". Propositions like Russell's "axiom of reducibility" are not logical propositions, and this explains our feeling that, if true, they can only be true by a happy chance.

6.1233　We can imagine a world in which the axiom of reducibility is not valid. But it is clear that logic has nothing to do with the question whether our world is really of this kind or not.

6.124　The logical propositions describe the scaffolding of the world, or rather they present it. They "treat" of nothing. They presuppose that names have meaning, and that elementary propositions have sense. And this is their connexion with the world. It is clear that it must show something about the world that certain combinations of symbols—which essentially have a definite character—are tautologies. Herein lies the decisive point. We said that in the symbols which we use much is arbitrary, much not. In logic only this expresses: but this means that in logic it is not *we* who express, by means of signs, what we want, but in logic the nature of the essentially necessary signs itself asserts. That is to say, if we know the logical syntax of any sign language, then all the propositions of logic are already given.

6.125　It is possible, even in the old logic, to give at the outset a description of all "true" logical propositions.

6.1251 Hence there can *never* be surprises in logic.

6.126 Whether a proposition belongs to logic can be determined by
determining the logical properties of the *symbol*.
And this we do when we prove a logical proposition. For
without troubling ourselves about a sense and a meaning, we
form the logical propositions out of others by mere *symbolic
rules*.
We prove a logical proposition by creating it out of other
logical propositions by applying in succession certain operations,
which again generate tautologies out of the first. (And from a
tautology only tautologies *follow*.)
Naturally this way of showing that its propositions are tautologies is quite unessential to logic. Because the propositions,
from which the proof starts, must show without proof that they
are tautologies.

6.1261 In logic process and result are equivalent. (Therefore no surprises.)

6.1262 Proof in logic is only a mechanical expedient to facilitate the
recognition of tautology, where it is complicated.

6.1263 It would be too remarkable, if one could prove a significant proposition *logically* from another, and a logical proposition *also*. It
is clear from the beginning that the logical proof of a significant
proposition and the proof *in* logic must be two quite different
things.

6.1264 The significant proposition asserts something, and its proof
shows that it is so; in logic every proposition is the form of a
proof.
Every proposition of logic is a modus ponens presented in
signs. (And the modus ponens can not be expressed by a proposition.)

6.1265 Logic can always be conceived to be such that every proposition
is its own proof.

6.127 All propositions of logic are of equal rank; there are not some
which are essentially primitive and others deduced from these.
Every tautology itself shows that it is a tautology.

6.1271   It is clear that the number of "primitive propositions of logic" is arbitrary, for we could deduce logic from one primitive proposition by simply forming, for example, the logical product of Frege's primitive propositions. (Frege would perhaps say that this would no longer be immediately self-evident. But it is remarkable that so exact a thinker as Frege should have appealed to the degree of self-evidence as the criterion of a logical proposition.)

6.13   Logic is not a theory but a reflexion of the world.

Logic is transcendental.

6.2   Mathematics is a logical method.

The propositions of mathematics are equations, and therefore pseudo-propositions.

6.21   Mathematical propositions express no thoughts.

6.211   In life it is never a mathematical proposition which we need, but we use mathematical propositions *only* in order to infer from propositions which do not belong to mathematics to others which equally do not belong to mathematics.

(In philosophy the question "Why do we really use that word, that proposition?" constantly leads to valuable results.)

6.22   The logic of the world which the propositions of logic show in tautologies, mathematics shows in equations.

6.23   If two expressions are connected by the sign of equality, this means that they can be substituted for one another. But whether this is the case must show itself in the two expressions themselves.

It characterizes the logical form of two expressions, that they can be substituted for one another.

6.231   It is a property of affirmation that it can be conceived as double denial.

It is a property of "$1 + 1 + 1 + 1$" that it can be conceived as "$(1 + 1) + (1 + 1)$".

6.232   Frege says that these expressions have the same meaning but different senses.

But what is essential about equation is that it is not necessary in order to show that both expressions, which are connected by the sign of equality, have the same meaning: for this can be perceived from the two expressions themselves.

6.2321 And, that the propositions of mathematics can be proved means nothing else than that their correctness can be seen without our having to compare what they express with the facts as regards correctness.

6.2322 The identity of the meaning of two expressions cannot be *asserted*. For in order to be able to assert anything about their meaning, I must know their meaning, and if I know their meaning, I know whether they mean the same or something different.

6.2323 The equation characterizes only the standpoint from which I consider the two expressions, that is to say the standpoint of their equality of meaning.

6.233 To the question whether we need intuition for the solution of mathematical problems it must be answered that language itself here supplies the necessary intuition.

6.2331 The process of calculation brings about just this intuition.

Calculation is not an experiment.

6.234 Mathematics is a method of logic.

6.2341 The essential of mathematical method is working with equations. On this method depends the fact that every proposition of mathematics must be self-intelligible.

6.24 The method by which mathematics arrives at its equations is the method of substitution.

For equations express the substitutability of two expressions, and we proceed from a number of equations to new equations, replacing expressions by others in accordance with the equations.

6.241 Thus the proof of the proposition $2 \times 2 = 4$ runs:

$$(\Omega^\nu)^{\mu\prime}x = \Omega^{\nu\times\mu\prime}x \text{ Def.}$$
$$\Omega^{2\times2\prime}x = (\Omega^2)^{2\prime}x = (\Omega^2)^{1+1\prime}x = \Omega^{2\prime}\Omega^{2\prime}x = \Omega^{1+1\prime}\Omega^{1+1\prime}x$$
$$= (\Omega'\Omega)'(\Omega'\Omega)'x = \Omega'\Omega'\Omega'\Omega'x = \Omega^{1+1+1+1\prime}x = \Omega^{4\prime}x.$$

6.3 Logical research means the investigation of *all regularity*. And outside logic all is accident.

6.31 The so-called law of induction cannot in any case be a logical law, for it is obviously a significant proposition.—And therefore it cannot be a law a priori either.

6.32 The law of causality is not a law but the form of a law.*

6.321 "Law of Causality" is a class name. And as in mechanics there are, for instance, minimum-laws, such as that of least action, so in physics there are causal laws, laws of the causality form.

6.3211 Men had indeed an idea that there must be a "law of least action", before they knew exactly how it ran. (Here, as always, the a priori certain proves to be something purely logical.)

6.33 We do not *believe* a priori in a law of conservation, but we *know* a priori the possibility of a logical form.

6.34 All propositions, such as the law of causation, the law of continuity in nature, the law of least expenditure in nature, etc. etc., all these are a priori intuitions of possible forms of the propositions of science.

6.341 Newtonian mechanics, for example, brings the description of the universe to a unified form. Let us imagine a white surface with irregular black spots. We now say: Whatever kind of picture these make I can always get as near as I like to its description, if I cover the surface with a sufficiently fine square network and now say of every square that it is white or black. In this way I shall have brought the description of the surface to a unified form. This form is arbitrary, because I could have applied with equal success a net with a triangular or hexagonal mesh. It can happen that the description would have been simpler with the aid of a triangular mesh; that is to say we might have described the surface more accurately with a triangular, and coarser, than with the finer square mesh, or vice versa, and so on. To the different networks correspond different systems of describing the world. Mechanics determine a form of description by saying: All propositions in the description of the world must be obtained in a given way from a number of given propositions—the mechanical axioms. It thus provides the bricks for building the edifice of science, and says: Whatever building thou wouldst erect, thou

* *I.e.* not the form of one particular law, but of any law of a certain sort (B. R.).

shalt construct it in some manner with these bricks and these alone.

(As with the system of numbers one must be able to write down any arbitrary number, so with the system of mechanics one must be able to write down any arbitrary physical proposition.)

6.342 And now we see the relative position of logic and mechanics. (We could construct the network out of figures of different kinds, as out of triangles and hexagons together.) That a picture like that instanced above can be described by a network of a given form asserts *nothing* about the picture. (For this holds of every picture of this kind.) But *this* does characterize the picture, the fact, namely, that it can be *completely* described by a definite net of *definite* fineness.

So too the fact that it can be described by Newtonian mechanics asserts nothing about the world; but *this* asserts something, namely, that it can be described in that particular way in which it is described, as is indeed the case. The fact, too, that it can be described more simply by one system of mechanics than by another says something about the world.

6.343 Mechanics is an attempt to construct according to a single plan all *true* propositions which we need for the description of the world.

6.3431 Through the whole apparatus of logic the physical laws still speak of the objects of the world.

6.3432 We must not forget that the description of the world by mechanics is always quite general. There is, for example, never any mention of *particular* material points in it, but always only of *some points or other*.

6.35 Although the spots in our picture are geometrical figures, geometry can obviously say nothing about their actual form and position. But the network is *purely* geometrical, and all its properties can be given a priori.

Laws, like the law of causation, etc., treat of the network and not of what the network described.

6.36 If there were a law of causality, it might run: "There are natural laws".

But that can clearly not be said: it shows itself.

6.361 In the terminology of Hertz we might say: Only *uniform* connexions are *thinkable*.

6.3611 We cannot compare any process with the "passage of time"—there is no such thing—but only with another process (say, with the movement of the chronometer).

Hence the description of the temporal sequence of events is only possible if we support ourselves on another process.

It is exactly analogous for space. When, for example, we say that neither of two events (which mutually exclude one another) can occur, because there is *no cause* why the one should occur rather than the other, it is really a matter of our being unable to describe *one* of the two events unless there is some sort of asymmetry. And if there *is* such an asymmetry, we can regard this as the *cause* of the occurrence of the one and of the non-occurrence of the other.

6.36111 The Kantian problem of the right and left hand which cannot be made to cover one another already exists in the plane, and even in one-dimensional space; where the two congruent figures *a* and *b* cannot be made to cover one another without moving them out of this space. The right and left hand are in fact completely congruent. And the fact that they cannot be made to cover one another has nothing to do with it.

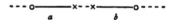

A right-hand glove could be put on a left hand if it could be turned round in four-dimensional space.

6.362 What can be described can happen too, and what is excluded by the law of causality cannot be described.

6.363 The process of induction is the process of assuming the *simplest* law that can be made to harmonize with our experience.

6.3631 This process, however, has no logical foundation but only a psychological one.

It is clear that there are no grounds for believing that the simplest course of events will really happen.

6.36311 That the sun will rise to-morrow, is an hypothesis; and that means that we do not *know* whether it will rise.

6.37 A necessity for one thing to happen because another has happened does not exist. There is only *logical* necessity.

6.371 At the basis of the whole modern view of the world lies the illusion that the so-called laws of nature are the explanations of natural phenomena.

6.372 So people stop short at natural laws as at something unassailable, as did the ancients at God and Fate.

And they both are right and wrong. But the ancients were clearer, in so far as they recognized one clear conclusion, whereas in the modern system it should appear as though *everything* were explained.

6.373 The world is independent of my will.

6.374 Even if everything we wished were to happen, this would only be, so to speak, a favour of fate, for there is no *logical* connexion between will and world, which would guarantee this, and the assumed physical connexion itself we could not again will.

6.375 As there is only a *logical* necessity, so there is only a *logical* impossibility.

6.3751 For two colours, *e.g.* to be at one place in the visual field, is impossible, logically impossible, for it is excluded by the logical structure of colour.

Let us consider how this contradiction presents itself in physics. Somewhat as follows: That a particle cannot at the same time have two velocities, *i.e.* that at the same time it cannot be in two places, *i.e.* that particles in different places at the same time cannot be identical.

(It is clear that the logical product of two elementary propositions can neither be a tautology nor a contradiction. The assertion that a point in the visual field has two different colours at the same time, is a contradiction.)

6.4 All propositions are of equal value.

6.41 The sense of the world must lie outside the world. In the world everything is as it is and happens as it does happen. *In* it there is no value—and if there were, it would be of no value.

If there is a value which is of value, it must lie outside all happening and being-so. For all happening and being-so is accidental.

What makes it non-accidental cannot lie *in* the world, for otherwise this would again be accidental.

It must lie outside the world.

6.42 Hence also there can be no ethical propositions.

Propositions cannot express anything higher.

6.421 It is clear that ethics cannot be expressed.

Ethics are transcendental.

(Ethics and æsthetics are one.)

6.422 The first thought in setting up an ethical law of the form "thou shalt ..." is: And what if I do not do it. But it is clear that ethics has nothing to do with punishment and reward in the ordinary sense. This question as to the *consequences* of an action must therefore be irrelevant. At least these consequences will not be events. For there must be something right in that formulation of the question. There must be some sort of ethical reward and ethical punishment, but this must lie in the action itself.

(And this is clear also that the reward must be something acceptable, and the punishment something unacceptable.)

6.423 Of the will as the bearer of the ethical we cannot speak.

And the will as a phenomenon is only of interest to psychology.

6.43 If good or bad willing changes the world, it can only change the limits of the world, not the facts; not the things that can be expressed in language.

In brief, the world must thereby become quite another. It must so to speak wax or wane as a whole.

The world of the happy is quite another than that of the unhappy.

6.431 As in death, too, the world does not change, but ceases.

6.4311 Death is not an event of life. Death is not lived through.

If by eternity is understood not endless temporal duration but timelessness, then he lives eternally who lives in the present.

Our life is endless in the way that our visual field is without limit.

6.4312   The temporal immortality of the soul of man, that is to say, its eternal survival also after death, is not only in no way guaranteed, but this assumption in the first place will not do for us what we always tried to make it do. Is a riddle solved by the fact that I survive for ever? Is this eternal life not as enigmatic as our present one? The solution of the riddle of life in space and time lies *outside* space and time.

(It is not problems of natural science which have to be solved.)

6.432   *How* the world is, is completely indifferent for what is higher. God does not reveal himself *in* the world.

6.4321   The facts all belong only to the task and not to its performance.

6.44   Not *how* the world is, is the mystical, but *that* it is.

6.45   The contemplation of the world sub specie aeterni is its contemplation as a limited whole.

The feeling of the world as a limited whole is the mystical feeling.

6.5   For an answer which cannot be expressed the question too cannot be expressed.

The riddle does not exist.

If a question can be put at all, then it *can* also be answered.

6.51   Scepticism is *not* irrefutable, but palpably senseless, if it would doubt where a question cannot be asked.

For doubt can only exist where there is a question; a question only where there is an answer, and this only where something *can* be *said*.

6.52   We feel that even if *all possible* scientific questions be answered, the problems of life have still not been touched at all. Of course there is then no question left, and just this is the answer.

6.521   The solution of the problem of life is seen in the vanishing of this problem.

(Is not this the reason why men to whom after long doubting

the sense of life became clear, could not then say wherein this sense consisted?)

6.522 There is indeed the inexpressible. This *shows* itself; it is the mystical.

6.53 The right method of philosophy would be this. To say nothing except what can be said, *i.e.* the propositions of natural science, *i.e.* something that has nothing to do with philosophy: and then always, when someone else wished to say something metaphysical, to demonstrate to him that he had given no meaning to certain signs in his propositions. This method would be unsatisfying to the other—he would not have the feeling that we were teaching him philosophy—but it would be the only strictly correct method.

6.54 My propositions are elucidatory in this way: he who understands me finally recognizes them as senseless, when he has climbed out through them, on them, over them. (He must so to speak throw away the ladder, after he has climbed up on it.)

He must surmount these propositions; then he sees the world rightly.

7 Whereof one cannot speak, thereof one must be silent.